Praise for Nawang Khechog's
Awakening Kindness

"Nawang Khechog is a dedicated student of the Dalai Lama, and I have worked with him several times through the PeaceJam program as he has shared his philosophy of kindness with the youth of the world. I hope and pray that this book will benefit many people by helping to inspire kindness and compassion in their hearts.
We need more books like this today!"

Archbishop Desmond Tutu, 1984 Nobel Peace Laureate

"Nawang Khechog beautifully shares with us his understanding of wisdom, kindness, and compassion. Through experiences in his life, he shows us that how we cope with change is important and can help us reach our full potential as kind and compassionate human beings. Anyone seeking a deeper understanding of these values will benefit greatly from reading his work."

Jody Williams, 1997 Nobel Peace Laureate
and Chair, Nobel Women's Initiative

"Nawang Khechog not only writes about awakening kindness, he has lived that awakening, humbly, thoroughly, and creatively. Given the tenor of our times, these teachings are extremely important."

Michael Bernard Beckwith, author of *Spiritual Liberation*

"*Awakening Kindness* is so very joyous and deeply spiritual—the written compassion infolds and holds you. Thank you, Nawang Khechog—His Holiness the Dalai Lama has polished the diamond that is your karma."

Betty Williams, 1979 Nobel Peace Laureate

"Awakening Kindness is an inspiring and practical guide to nurture and nourish the expression of kindness and compassion in every day life. By presenting many simple exercises and documenting the powerful examples of many ordinary citizens and Nobel peace prize laureates, Nawang Khechog invites us to practice kindness. Anyone who picks up this book and is receptive to its message will immediately enjoy the many benefits of living in this simple and sacred way."

Richard J. Davidson, William James and Vilas Research Professor of Psychology and Psychiatry, and Director for the Center for Investigating Healthy Minds, University of Wisconsin–Madison

"As a good friend of Nawang Khechog's for many years, I've seen him transform some enormous life challenges into a solid commitment to be of service to others. Under the guidance of some of Tibet's greatest teachers, his main practice, during his four years as a hermit meditator and thirty-something years as a practitioner, has been one of universal love, compassion, and Bodhicitta. I hope that his book, *Awakening Kindness*, will inspire people to practice and cultivate these inner values, and achieve a lasting happiness for themselves."

Richard Gere, actor and activist

"Nawang Khechog's beautiful book really does awaken kindness— in our hearts, in others who respond, and in the world. He is a deeply spiritual player upon the magic flute of love and compassion in action. Here his melody comes through in words. I am inspired by his book and I heartily recommend it to you."

Robert Thurman, author of *Why the Dalai Lama Matters* and cofounder of Tibet House US

Awakening Kindness

Finding Joy Through Compassion for Others

NAWANG KHECHOG

FOREWORD BY
HIS HOLINESS THE DALAI LAMA

ATRIA BOOKS
New York London Toronto Sydney

BEYOND WORDS
Hillsboro, Oregon

ATRIA BOOKS
A Division of Simon & Schuster, Inc.
1230 Avenue of the Americas
New York, NY 10020

BEYOND WORDS
20827 N.W. Cornell Road, Suite 500
Hillsboro, Oregon 97124-9808
503-531-8700 / 503-531-8773 fax
www.beyondword.com

Copyright © 2010 by Nawang Khechog

Managing editor: Lindsay S. Brown
Editors: Gretchen Stelter and Ali McCart
Proofreader: Jade Chan
Design: Devon Smith
Composition: William H. Brunson Typography Services
Music download courtesy of Sounds True, Inc.

First Atria Books/Beyond Words hardcover edition December 2010

ATRIA BOOKS and colophon are trademarks of Simon & Schuster, Inc.
Beyond Words Publishing is a division of Simon & Schuster, Inc.

For more information about special discounts for bulk purchases,
please contact Simon & Schuster Special Sales at 1-866-506-1949 or
business@simonandschuster.com.

The Simon & Schuster Speakers Bureau can bring authors to your live event.
For more information or to book an event, contact the Simon & Schuster Speakers
Bureau at 1-866-248-3049 or visit our website at www.simonspeakers.com.

Manufactured in the United States of America

10 9 8 7 6 5 4 3 2 1

Library of Congress Cataloging-in-Publication Data

Khechog, Nawang.
    Awakening kindness : finding joy through compassion for others / Nawang Khechog.
        p.   cm.
    1. Kindness.   2. Compassion.   3. Love.   I. Title.
    BJ1533.K5K44   2010
    177'.7—dc22

                                                                        2010027169

ISBN: 978-1-58270-252-0
ISBN: 978-1-4391-6403-7 (ebook)

The corporate mission of Beyond Words Publishing, Inc.: *Inspire to Integrity*

*This book is dedicated to the long life of
His Holiness the Dalai Lama and to fulfilling his
wish to inspire humanity toward a kind
and compassionate society.*

Contents

THE DALAI LAMA

FOREWORD

All sentient beings are fundamentally the same, because we all want to be happy, and none of us wants to be miserable. Therefore, it is really worthwhile trying to discover how we can bring about genuine, lasting happiness.

This begins when we begin to look beyond our narrow self-interest to find out and consider what is of interest and benefit to others. As social animals dependent on others around us, warm-heartedness and affection have a powerful effect. Affection recognizes others as our brothers and sisters. Similarly, honesty and a truthful, concerned attitude bring about trust. Trust brings harmony, and harmony brings about a happier society.

In this book Nawang Khechog explains the need for kindness in our lives and ways people can use to develop it. Nawang was born in Tibet and as part of his education spent some time quietly as a meditator in the hills above Dharamsala, after which he became known worldwide as a musician. I commend him for his efforts to awaken others to the understanding that, as a source of lasting happiness and joy, kindness and compassion are among the principal things that make our lives meaningful.

19 July 2010

CHANGE STARTS HERE PeaceJam.org

Dear Nobel Peace Laureates,

Ivan and I have worked with Nawang Khechog since 1996, when we started the PeaceJam program. He has always been very supportive of PeaceJam's work and vision. The last ten years he has presented his kindness workshop "Peace through Kindness" to the PeaceJam youth, led kindness meditation for the annual national affiliate directors retreat, and performed his peace music to open the public addresses by many of the Noble Peace Laureates at PeaceJam conferences, including at the public address by all ten Noble Peace Laureates at the 10th anniversary in Denver Colorado, 2006.

The last twenty years Nawang has always used his kindness prayer "May All Be Kind to Each Other" before every one of his musical performances and at his kindness workshops. He has used this kindness prayer at the U.N General Assembly Hall during his opening performance for the first Earth Summit Precom gathering, as well as at Carnegie Hall and RFK Stadium Concerts, and at maximum security prison where he gave Kindness Workshops and a Musical Offering.

Nawang was involved in a horrible car accident last year that took the life of his niece and nearly claimed his own as well. We are very happy that he is still here with us and very impressed by his quick recovery. Despite this horrific event he is still as kind, loving and gracious as ever, which shows the nature of his heart.

Based on his kindness prayer "May All Be Kind to Each Other" he has created Walking Kindness, Dance of Universal Kindness, Embracing Kindness, and Kindness Meditation and Chanting. Although Nawang's innovative kindness tools are very simple and down to earth, over the years we have witnessed them to be quite effective for inspiring kindness. We value and support his work and therefore we request that all of the Noble Peace Laureates on the PeaceJam board to please consider blessing and endorsing Nawang Khechog's kindness prayer "May All Be Kind to Each Other by placing your signature below. We sincerely thank you for your consideration.

Warmest regards,
Dawn Engle   Ivan Suvanjieff

Executive Director   President/CEO

Archbishop Desmond Tutu   **President Jose Ramos Horta**   **Rigoberta Menchu Tum**

Judy Williams   **The Dalai Lama**   **Betty Williams**   **Shirin Ebadi**

Adolfo Perez Esquivel   **President Oscar Arias**   **Mairead Corrigan Maguire**

CHANGE STARTS HERE PeaceJam.org

x

1

From the Beginning: An Introduction

I have been very fortunate in having many great teachers in my life, especially His Holiness the Dalai Lama. I have had the privilege of studying, meditating on, and experiencing kindness from an early age. As an artist and musician who has been exposed to modern culture and lived in the West these twenty-some years, I have become quite familiar with the contemporary way of life and ways of thinking. Given this background, I have come up with some creative ways to share the essence of spirituality, especially when discussing contemplative fields like meditation, wisdom, compassion, and kindness.

My duty with this book is to introduce some essential points on wisdom and compassion in a creative, accessible, and practical way. It is much like an opening act for a concert—I'm here to introduce the main act to the audience. If people are inspired to experience deeper teachings along the same lines, then they can stay for the main act. Likewise, if people are inspired by what they learn of kindness in this book, then they can study the great masters, just as concertgoers would seek more concerts and performers to further enhance their experience. There are many great teachers available around the world, like His Holiness the Dalai Lama. While I am not qualified to be a lama, I am not needed in that capacity, and I am more useful to the general public as a medium for sharing kindness and wisdom.

I am a spiritual friend when I'm teaching. I try to share what I have learned about spiritual values as well as the experiences I have had over the years while trying to practice their teachings. I'm hoping you will feel some of those spiritual values while reading this book. I'm truly hoping that understanding the events in my life and knowing some of my experiences will make you feel as if I'm your spiritual friend as I share with you what others have taught me and what I have awakened to.

Early Life

One specific occurrence before I was born and one very early in my life inspired me, setting my life on the path I now follow. One was the Communist Chinese invasion of Tibet. The other was a yogi—a hermit meditator—who visited my family when I was two or three years old. The yogi was traveling through Tibet from the Golog, Amdo, region—where the Dalai Lama was born—all the way to central Tibet by doing prostrations. My family's only possessions were a tent made out of yak hair, yaks, and other basic nomadic necessities, but this yogi chose to stay with us. Though we didn't have heat or any sort of luxuries, our tradition was to invite in any lamas or hermit meditators who came through, treat them well, give them the food and the shelter we could, and so on. So he stayed with my family over four or five days, and at night he would stay up and chant prayers. One night, he asked my father to stay up with him, and he told my father that times were going to get worse in Tibet and that we should go to India. My family took his advice, and by the time I was six, in 1959, we were living in India as refugees.

All that has happened in my life since then has been partly because of that yogi. He blessed me with freedom and adventures; he helped me realize the opportunity to do all the things in this world I have experienced. I sometimes feel he might have been an emanation of Chenrezig, Buddha of love and compassion, who came to bless my entire family, and I am forever indebted to this saint for the way he altered my life path.

Because of this yogi and the Communist Chinese invasion of Tibet, I've been given the opportunity to play peaceful music, share my creativity, and talk about the value of kindness and the ancient teachings of wisdom and compassion with people around the world. I've also met His Holiness the Dalai Lama, the greatest teacher of love, compassion, kindness, and wisdom. Because of all this, I look on the invasion of Tibet as a blessing in disguise, and I feel truly inspired by the yogi from my youth.

Invasion of Tibet

The invasion of Tibet changed many lives in devastating ways. What happened to my country, to the Tibetan people, is truly tragic. More than one million Tibetans died, and over six thousand monasteries were destroyed at the hands of Chinese authorities. For the whole of Tibet, it is the most unfortunate moment in more than two thousand years of history.

Vast destruction has continued over many years, including the demolition of wildlife and the environment, and it has not ended. Most threatening for the survival of Tibetan civilization and cultural identity are the millions of Chinese that have moved into Tibet. This is China's ultimate insidious plan—to destroy Tibetan identity by overwhelming Tibetan resistance.

But what Chinese authorities do not realize is that the Dalai Lama and the Tibetan culture of nonviolence and compassion have won the hearts of people around the world—including our peace-loving and spiritual Chinese brothers and sisters. Members of the younger Tibetan generation are also inspired, and they are determined to preserve our culture and to carry on the just and nonviolent Tibetan freedom struggle forever— no matter how many generations it may take. Therefore, I have every hope that Tibetan culture and civilization will never die.

◎   ◎   ◎

If you look at the invasion of Tibet from a positive place, the world is now able to experience the wisdom and the teachings of the Dalai Lama. His teachings around the world spread the value of tolerance and love, and they are a blessing; the world is now exposed to Tibetan Buddhist teachings and the path to awakening kindness.

In Tibetan spiritual tradition, we say, "Transform all problems and hardships into higher spiritual elevation." This is very useful and inspiring when we are going through rough times, especially in the twenty-first century. If we can see how a positive outlook and the spirit of forgiveness, kindness, and compassion are of the highest value when we approach difficult situations, then we can all truly benefit from any situation, whether of personal, national, or global scope. Some of the highest examples of such a reality are great beings like Gandhi, Mother Teresa, Archbishop Desmond Tutu, Betty Williams, His Holiness the Dalai Lama, and all the Nobel Peace Laureates.

I feel that even I benefited from living in Chandragiri, Orissa—our Tibetan refugee camp in India. When I was a young teenager, several other boys my age and I were inspired to become monks because of one great lama who visited. I had no idea what it meant to be a monk, but a deep spirituality inside me inspired me to pursue it, and I was excited.

At that time, my father was not living with us (he was doing roadwork in Chamba Valley, Himachal Pradesh, India), so the decision regarding my monkhood was left to my mother. I pleaded with her, and initially she refused. This had quite a bit to do with Tibetan tradition. When a man becomes a monk, he leaves his family and can no longer help support them. Because I was the only son, my family relied on me very much, so my desire to become a monk was a serious matter. It didn't just affect my life; it affected my entire family. But I begged for months, and eventually my mother's kindness and understanding changed her decision. So, at the age of thirteen, I began my studies as a monk.

His Holiness the Dalai Lama

Though it defied our nonviolent culture, many young Tibetan people joined the army, and after I began my studies as a monk, I ran away to join the Tibetan guerilla army as well. While I was in the army, I had no idea how to meditate, how to cultivate the inner values important to Buddhism, or how to live a happy life in general. Because of the discord between my guerilla lifestyle and Buddhist beliefs, I believed that meditating on Buddhist values was even more important than it would have been otherwise. When I was introduced to two scriptures, called *Lamrim* and *Koonsang Lamae Shel-loong*, I started this practice of meditation on my own. Gradually, the practice started to affect me, and all I wanted to do was become a hermit meditator, like many other great monks and the yogi who had helped set me on my life path. I began to realize how truly important the spiritual values of universal love, kindness, and inner wisdom are, and I wanted to meditate on and cultivate these inner qualities full time.

Right after I made the decision to become a hermit meditator, when I was about eighteen years old, I found out that the Dalai Lama was traveling to Mussoorie, Uttarakhand, India, and I tried to get an audience with him to ask him for guidance. During his visit, though, his principal private secretary, Kuno Tarak-la—another great practitioner—told me that I was too young to say for sure what I wanted to do with my life. He told me to contemplate and we would see. Two years later, Kuno Tarak-la wrote me a letter informing me that I could go to Dharamsala, where the Dalai Lama lives, and have my audience.

When I received the letter, I still didn't have any desire other than to be a hermit meditator, so I made the decision to go to Dharamsala to finally speak with His Holiness the Dalai Lama. I had some rupees, the few I could get from the army, and the clothes I could fit in my bag, and I left the army. In my mind, I had left it forever, even though it was illegal. I only got ten days' leave—called casual leave—but I left and went to Dharamsala. When I got there, I told His Holiness that I wanted to begin living as a hermit meditator, and I asked the Dalai Lama to guide me. His Holiness accepted me as his student and ended up sponsoring me, which entailed guiding me for the four years that I was living in the mountains.

The Dalai Lama is the preeminent Tibetan Buddhist teacher in the world; whether you're in Tibet, India, Mongolia, or any other part of the world where Tibetan Buddhism is practiced, the Dalai Lama is the most highly respected teacher, so in one way he already was my ultimate teacher. He is also the supreme secular and spiritual leader of Tibet. Though the Dalai Lama says, "I'm just a simple Buddhist monk," we believe he is the reincarnation of the Buddha of compassion.

Chenrezig, Buddha of
Love and Compassion

In Tibetan Buddhism, we have many ancient legends set thousands of years from Buddha Shakyamuni's time, and in the seventh century the great master Padma Sambava—who helped establish Buddhism in Tibet and was a great saint—prophesized what would happen in Tibet when China took over. The prophesy spoke of the great monk who would lead Tibet during that time and would be an emanation of Padma Sambava. I heard a beautiful legend while doing a Buddhist teaching. It was called *Kadam Fachoe Buchoe*, which means "The Doctrine of Father and Son." It's a beautiful story that goes back to Buddha's time and beyond, and it clarifies that the incarnations of the Dalai Lama are emanations of the Buddha of Compassion.

⊚　⊚　⊚

The current incarnation, Tenzin Gyatso, the fourteenth Dalai Lama, is one of the few Buddhist scholars to study not only from one tradition but from all four of the great Buddhist traditions: Nyingma, Sakya, Kagyu, and Geluk—the tradition that His Holiness belongs to. The Dalai Lama has been able to study with some of the greatest masters of our time, including Dilgo Khyentse Rinpoche, Kalu Rinpoche, Chogye Trichen Rinpoche, Myenling Trichen Rinpoche, Trulshik Rinpoche, Khunu Lama Rinpoche, and Gen Nima Rinpoche. Two of his most influential tutors were the well-known great masters Ling Rinpoche and Trijang Rinpoche. The Dalai Lama is able to study hundreds of different scriptures; therefore, he's able to teach from all these different Buddhist traditions. There is no master of all four traditions like the Dalai Lama, so his knowledge is beyond that of all other Buddhist teachers. In all these ways, the Dalai Lama is an incredible, compassionate, wise teacher, and none can compare.

Being personally sponsored by His Holiness the Dalai Lama—inarguably the greatest living Tibetan master and the current incarnation of the Buddha of Compassion—and being guided by him brought a complete evolution in my life. For the next four years, I fully focused on being a hermit meditator. In general, Tibetan hermit meditators focus on two things. I like to say that Buddhism isn't so much a religion as it is a way of life—a philosophy—and individuals who believe in this basically try to do two things: they try to become wiser, and they try to become more compassionate. That's it—

kindness and compassion combined with wisdom. If we are wise but not kind, then we're in trouble, so it's important to have both together. When acting in kindness, living life in general, and even while reading this book, we need both wisdom and compassion.

To understand this more fully, think of an eagle. When the eagle wants to fly, it needs two wings. With two wings, it can soar beautifully. In the same way, individuals have to become very wise on one side and kind on the other. When we do that, we can gradually become greater human beings and greater citizens of humanity, and our journey in life becomes more peaceful. This is why all Buddhist practitioners try to become wiser on one side and more compassionate and kinder on the other. This means, of course, that while meditating in the mountains, I contemplated and tried to become both. I still try to focus on these values and nurture them in my heart every day.

When Buddhists focus on gaining wisdom, we often contemplate the transitory and interdependent nature of life; part of being wise is understanding the many changes that affect our lives and that our behavior affects others' lives. Buddha said, "*Due jay thamche mitakpa*," which means that any reality whose mode of existence depends on causes and conditions is bound to change.

The Transitory Nature of Life

Life is transitory. This is an important foundation of Buddhism as well as universal wisdom. Things constantly change, and the effects of these changes are what guide us on our path through life. Everyone's life is affected by changes far outside his or her control, but it is what one does when things change that shows who we really can be and makes us live up to our true potential. These changes outside our control should be looked on with kindness. When we accept that all things must eventually change, we can find the blessing in them, and then we can begin to view these changes—both in our life as well as in the world—as positive.

The interdependent nature of life is what shows us that our actions affect everyone and that focusing on just ourselves is dangerous. One of the teachings in Buddhism is to transcend and transform the egocentric mind, what is often called the "me-first" culture in the West. This me-first culture creates so much trouble in the world and in everyday life. When we become too focused on "me, me, me, me," we fail to recognize those around us and that they are on their own journeys, and especially that our selfish actions affect their journeys, often making them more difficult. To transcend the egocentric state of mind, one should follow the Buddhist teaching called

Shunyata, or "dependent origination." This wisdom focuses on how everything is interdependent; nothing is on its own. We sometimes become too focused on being the center—of the universe or just attention—but that's an exaggeration of our ego mind; it is not possible to be the center. To transcend this, we focus on the Buddhist teaching about the interdependent nature of life.

The Interdependent Nature of Life

We all depend on the life, nature, and acts of others. This tenet of Buddhist belief relates to reincarnation as well, as we believe that any sentient being could be the new incarnation of someone we have cared deeply for. Even if this is not part of your belief system, it is hard to deny that all life depends on the survival of other life. Scientifically, we can see how plant and animal life have sustained us for aeons, from food and clothing to the basic lifeblood of oxygen. When we see how all living things depend on other living things to survive—therefore we all depend on each other—it becomes clear how much of an impact our actions have on everything around us. This clearly illustrates the importance of consideration and care with all life.

As a monk, I meditated on these inner values, and I still do my best to take these teachings into my heart and practice;

however, my main practice was and will always remain universal love and compassion. These values make up one of the Dalai Lama's main practices, too, and they are some of the most all-embracing spiritual values that can benefit all human beings—whether they are Buddhist or not. (In fact, they are completely independent of religion.) They can benefit any human being. For more than twenty years, I have been listening to teachings of the Dalai Lama in Western countries, and his main focus is always on love and compassion because it goes beyond all religion. Every being on Earth can benefit from this, which is why it is the focus of this book.

The Dalai Lama says, "When we are born on this earth, we don't have religion." Do dogs have religion? No. Do cats have religion? No. Do they need love and compassion? Yes. Every species on this planet needs love and compassion in their life. It's as simple as that. I try to follow in the footsteps of the Dalai Lama in sharing this with humanity, which is what my workshops, my music, and this book are for. All I'm trying to do is share the value of love and compassion. It is time to say to the world, "Love and compassion are valuable." We need to believe this and try to follow it. Becoming kind and compassionate is something everyone benefits from; that's what my journey and the lessons in my life have brought me here to share with you.

My Other Teachers

The Dalai Lama has often spoken of the fact that his first inspiration for being compassionate in this life came from his mother—not from Buddhist teaching. When we first come into this world, or are only one or two years old, we can't understand certain teachings. However, the moment the Dalai Lama was born, he was in his mother's care and love, nursed by his mother; that is the first inspiration he had that awakened the seed of love and compassion in his heart. And, as he has said, this would last him the rest of his life.

My mom was formerly a nun from the Drukpa Kagyu monastery, and I consider her the first spiritual teacher in my life. She told me stories of the Tibetan saint Milarepa—the most revered and respected saint in Tibet—and she sang me spiritual songs. Through these actions, my mother influenced me spiritually, and she also showed me the value of kindness. She was an exceptionally kind person; whenever any beggar came, she never sent him away empty-handed. We were very poor in exile, but she didn't care. Whenever she had something to give, she gave, and I will always remember how her kindness shone through her, inspired me, and touched the lives of many others. She was truly an embodiment of the value of kindness.

The last time I was in India visiting my family, I ran into a local Indian lady. I knew her from my childhood, and as we talked, she told me how much she missed my mom—who had passed away several years before—and her kindness. That was very touching for me, to see how long true kindness can leave its imprint.

My father is a different story, though. He taught me a disparate lesson concerning people and kindness. He was a Khampas, which is a specific warrior tribe in Tibet, and he lived up to it. Over the years, he softened, but when I was a child—and I could be very bad, so I don't blame him—he smacked me, quite badly sometimes. Little by little, he changed. One time, when I came home to visit my family, everyone was excited to tell me that someone had been giving my dad a hard time and wanted to fight, but my dad wouldn't; he had changed. I learned from my dad that human beings have the ability to transform, to become kinder. We can change; it is possible. With my father's example, I saw that teaching the value of kindness, sharing His Holiness the Dalai Lama's teachings, and following the path as best we can ourselves can bring about real change in people.

While the most important event in my life has been having a deep connection with His Holiness the Dalai Lama, all my teachers have affected my life. As a monk, I had two main mentors who were introduced to me by the Dalai Lama when I went to Dharamsala. They taught me values that are still with me and are part of what I share with others. One of my personal teachers was Kyabje Lati Rinpoche, a very humble, gentle, and patient teacher who was respected by many. When the Dalai Lama was being considered as the highest qualified Buddhist master—called *Geshe Lharampa*—he had to demonstrate to other Buddhist masters that he was an expert in his Buddhist studies, and Kyabje Lati Rinpoche was one of the masters he debated.

Kyabje Lati Rinpoche was one of the most respected and learned monks of his time in Tibet, and he became the abbot of Ganden Monastery while in exile. The Dalai Lama recommended that I study from Kyabje Lati Rinpoche, and this teacher had me study one of the greatest Buddhist teachings, *Lamrim Chenmo*, or "The Great Treatise on the Stages of the Path to Enlightenment."

Buddha's teachings fill one hundred volumes, but Atisha and then Lama Tsongkhapa wrote that all the teachings come down to three points called the three scopes of the Path to Enlightenment in *Lamrim Chenmo*. Anyone who wants to pursue Buddha's teachings can follow this grand spiritual path. Atisha and Lama Tsongkhapa put all of the Buddha's teachings into this one very beautiful scripture, and my teacher went over this teaching with me word by word. That was one of the greatest blessings I had from him.

My next teacher after Kyabje Lati Rinpoche was Gen Yeshe Topden. He taught me from *A Guide to the Bodhisattva Way of Life*, one of the highest and most beautiful teachings on how to cultivate universal love and compassion. Choejook Darti is one of the most extensive commentaries. Gen Yeshe Topden taught me this scripture word by word, every day, and that was another incredible blessing for me because he had been a hermit meditator in the mountains for many years. I was his first student since he'd moved to the mountains. He never wanted to have a student; he simply wanted to meditate every day. But he accepted me and taught me this alternate scripture, featuring one of the most effective teachings on how to cultivate universal love and compassion—*bodhicitta*. Gen Yeshe Topden is a Geshe Lharampa—most learned one—and he is still one of the most respected hermit meditators that I know; he is so down to earth, so simple, always so humble. Because of his humility, ordinary people might not notice that he is one of the most respected lamas.

All these teachers have helped me gain wisdom and respect and honor the value of kindness. For more than thirty years, I have also had the opportunity to learn all aspects of Buddha's teaching from His Holiness the Dalai Lama's public teachings in India and in the West. I feel so fortunate to be able to receive these profound and vast teachings.

These are some of the greatest influences in my life that nurtured a seed in me, in my heart. I don't consider myself a good practitioner. I am still a very basic student, still struggling, but the experiences with my family and the teachings of these great masters have imprinted me. I feel this imprint on my heart to follow the path, so I do so as much as I can, in my own way. It is my sincere hope that sharing these feelings, experiences, and thoughts with you will awaken and nurture a seed in your own heart.

Life after Monkhood

To become a monk is such a beautiful path, but even I chose not to remain a monk because of temptations and because of my own karma. I feel that perhaps this karma has influenced me to focus on my music, workshops, and this book—what I'm actually supposed to be doing in this life. I don't know how long it will take to overcome temptation, but I am definitely still wrestling with it, as it's one of the human conditions, but as a Buddhist, I believe that things I did in my past lives are constantly affecting what's happening to me in this life. After eleven years as a monk and four years as a hermit meditator, I contracted tuberculosis in the mountains, and I had to leave because of it.

I used to feel very ashamed and guilty that I was not able to continue on the path of monkhood that I'd begun. Sometimes I like to ask my friends here in the West, "Can you be a monk or a nun for one month?" The answer is normally no, and because I was a monk for eleven years in the twentieth century, I feel like I haven't done too badly. I try to give myself a little credit. I feel that I made the right decision to become a monk, and because I was a monk, I was able to get all this teaching from the Dalai Lama, my personal teachers—Kyabje Lati Rinpoche and Gen Yeshe Topden—and from many other teachers from different Tibetan traditions. After all that, it was a great decision. Even if I couldn't maintain it for my whole life, my time as a monk has laid a very good spiritual foundation for my life.

I have learned a lot from my earlier teachers as well as from many other people. When I became sick with tuberculosis and had to leave the mountains, I ended up discovering a very different lesson in unconditional love. In 1985 I was in Australia, where I married Leslie Christianson, a very kind and beautiful Australian woman. Together, we had two beautiful children: Sangye, our son, and Tenzin, our daughter. Mixed-race marriages are difficult because of cultural distinctions as well as differences in mentality and upbringing. In my case, our differences were even greater because I was an ex-monk and ex-hermit meditator with zero experience in modern life, so this experience was a completely new lesson in patience and understanding. Suddenly, I became a husband and a father; all kinds of responsibilities were being showered on me, and it was unbelievable. Learning this different aspect of tenderness was a blessing in spite of how hard my new responsibilities were. Of course, the children brought so much to my life as well; they are so beautiful. I learned a lot about life and took such an interesting path because of Leslie and Sangye and Tenzin.

After eight years, though, our marriage wasn't working, so we went our separate ways. While we were together in Australia, though, we helped establish the Australia Tibet Council—the most effective Tibet support group in Australia—with others who were dedicated to helping the situation in Tibet. Leslie eventually became the first national director, and she worked hard day and night to help establish the council as a sound and effective support for Tibetans.

Around this time, I began to play the flute everywhere, and people really started to take interest in my music. I realized that in playing my music, I had found a way to talk to people, so I informed Australians about the suffering of Tibetans and the destruction of Tibet, and I asked for their help. My deep belief in universal love and compassion and the peaceful nature of my flute music combined to create a medium through which I could share this information with humanity; people could use my music in their lives to become happier, more peaceful, and kinder. I toured throughout Australia, performing music and recording albums, utilizing my music as a way to draw attention to the situation in Tibet.

In 1991 my life was touched by serendipitous circumstances when Richard Gere walked into the first store in the United States to carry my album. Gere is the cofounder of the beautiful and great organization Tibet House, and he asked my friend Phelgye, the owner of the Tibetan store, about my music. Phelgye told him, "This is a Tibetan, Nawang Khechog, who plays the flute in Australia. This is his album." That year, Tibet House was organizing an event called Year of Tibet, so Richard Gere told the other organizers that he wanted to have me be part of the program, and they agreed.

When Tibet House asked me to attend the event, I was so excited, and I ended up touring throughout all 1991. The tour went really well, and during it I realized that the United States is such a huge country—this is the most powerful country in the world—so if I wanted to do anything to help Tibet, staying here would be a good first step. I felt like that was it—

I should stay here and share not only information about Tibet's struggle for freedom but also the message of kindness, love, and compassion, so I ended up making the United States my home.

◎ ◎ ◎

The many different stops along my life path remind me constantly of how quickly things change and how much others affect our life. As long as our reality depends on other factors, our understanding or intolerance—whichever it may be on any given day—affects every single day of our life. My life has gone in many different directions, but I have always been lucky enough to truly understand the kindness and wisdom that have surrounded me. And when my life hasn't been blessed with these things, I have learned so much about my own ability to maintain these positive feelings that I count myself lucky to have learned about human nature in general and my own nature more specifically.

One of the most positive and universal points of human nature is that everyone wants happiness; nobody wants suffering. Nobody wants problems or to get into the kind of trouble that we have gotten into the last few years, from war and national debt to global warming and the energy crisis. It's obvious that everybody wants to change these situations and to be free of hardship, but we need wake-up calls every so often when we are so driven by greed and violence that we forget what's important. We can see what has happened in the last several years—all the deceptions, the corporate greed, and the extreme selfishness and self-interest that have driven us to the economic meltdown and worldwide recession. I hope our situation can improve and that we can learn something from it. And with the transitory nature of things and the interdependent nature of reality, everything can change: a difficult situation can change into a good one. It's like music; with the composition of the music and the arrangement of instruments, the music can be really beautiful, but if the arrangement or the composition is disquieting, then due to its own conditions, the music is dark and menacing. Here today, the United States has a new leader who is a Nobel Peace Laureate with a great vision and energy. Furthering President Obama's outlook, we should look to kindness and compassion to help him guide us toward fulfilling our aspirations and bringing beauty to the world's situation.

Whether we believe in Buddha, Jesus Christ, Allah, Krishna, or God, with one voice, what we all say is that the nature of this higher being is all-knowing, all-loving, and all-powerful. These three qualities are always used to describe this higher being, whatever name we may assign to it. Therefore, 24/7, we are never alone; somebody is out there, looking out for us. If we can realize that, we are never without help and care. Whatever we call that higher being—and it is truly each individual's choice—there is this higher force in the universe that is looking after us. This is an amazing foundation for optimism and hope. This is a great reason to awaken to the value of kindness, to be caring, and to spread this compassion to others so that the world can begin to change in positive ways—so that we can individually change in positive ways. And now, let it begin with us, in our beautiful hearts.

May all be kind to each other.

2

An Introduction to
Awakening Kindness

This is my simple religion. There is no need for temples;
no need for complicated philosophy. Our own brain,
our own heart is our temple; the philosophy is kindness.
—His Holiness the Dalai Lama

Awakening Kindness is based on what His Holiness the Dalai Lama calls "human values," which enhance our inner values. Based on this vision, this book focuses on the values of love, compassion, and kindness—universal feelings. Kindness is the foundation of all great religions, even as it goes beyond all religions. Kindness—for yourself and for others—is not a concept that must be taught or a philosophy that has to be understood. Kindness is a simple, organic feeling that we need to awaken and grow in our hearts. We must first learn to be kind to ourselves so that we can show kindness and feel it toward others. It is a feeling that we recognize and know, that we are intimately familiar with from birth, and it is essential to first learn how to be kind to, and truly take care of, ourselves.

In general, the most important thing in life is our own well-being. If we have no shelter or food, if we are suffering from the elements or from sickness, our well-being is negatively affected. External means of living are very important to our physical well-being, but they're only one part of the story. The other part is our internal well-being—the state of our mind, whether our heart is kind or unkind, loving and compassionate or uncaring and cold. This makes all the difference when it comes to true, lasting happiness. We have to put the focus on love, compassion, and kindness. For that, you need to ask what you can do to nurture these positive feelings in your heart and allow them to grow, hopefully to the extent that your heart becomes universally loving and compassionate to all beings.

Every one of us has the capacity to love and be kind to all other sentient beings, but we often don't try to tap into our heart's full potential. We don't realize that we are only utilizing a small percentage of our heart's potential for love. How much goodwill and charity do you feel every day and for how many people? It may be very limited at the moment, and that's okay. That's why you have picked up this book, because you want to know how to expand that. Most of us have a handful of loved ones—family members and close friends—whom we actively feel kindness and love for on a daily basis. But if you set aside a little time whenever you can to contemplate the points we will cover here, then you can begin to transform.

By actively trying, we will be able to love in a much greater way, but we must also notice the conditions we sometimes put on our caring. For example, when someone is from a different country or practices a different religion, it can be a block to our kindness. Nationality, different belief systems, and a number of other differences are suddenly barriers for us, and we cannot go beyond them to truly show kindness and love. The world has seen this happen for centuries.

Unfortunately, this exact scenario has happened a lot in recent history, and it is still happening in many ways. A destructive feeling begins in each of us, as individuals—in our heart, religion, or some other aspect—and then we cannot be kind or show love to someone who is unlike us—Christian or Muslim or Hindu or another different faith. We have to remember that our love here is greater than our differences; altruism is greater than egoism.

All the religions of the world, while they may differ in other respects, unitedly proclaim that nothing lives in this world but Truth.
—Mahatma Gandhi

All kinds of causes adversely affect our understanding, and we have trouble expanding our hearts beyond these conditions so that we can become someone able to love all sentient beings regardless of faith, nationality, opinion, culture, and so on. We know the potential is there; it is just a matter of expanding it beyond this small box. The process starts with us; then it spreads to all the people in our family—either our blood relatives or the family we have made for ourselves. We must start by loving ourselves and then the people around us, and then we can begin to gradually expand our heart.

It starts with us and then continues to the small circle of ours. When we look at these groups of people influenced by our kindness, they are concentric circles, with us in the center, our loved ones in the innermost circle, then our friends, and then a bigger circle—maybe fellow citizens or those we share a religious fellowship with. But there's always a condition. Because our heart doesn't go beyond these conditions, because we always think of a difference between ourselves and others, we are unable to care about all beings as we care about ourselves. But think about why we take care of ourselves: because we have a natural instinct to avoid suffering. That's why I take care of myself, try to overcome problems, and find ways to be happy in life, because it's my natural instinct to want happiness. This is our universal declaration of basic human nature: I want happiness. I don't want suffering.

To get stuck in that box of conditions is a tragic situation. We have the ability to go beyond these barriers to our empathy, and this is one of the greatest gifts that human beings have: we can consciously open our hearts and become able to love greater humanity and all species.

When a child is born, the first thing she does is cry. That's the first universal declaration of human nature saying, "I don't want suffering!" Being taken from the warmth and comfort of the womb and suddenly thrust into a cold and foreign place is upsetting. And it is that first cry that shows our displeasure at our situation. We want to feel safe and loved, just as we were in the womb.

As soon as the mother nurses the baby, the child becomes quiet and peaceful. That's the second universal declaration of human nature saying, "Yes, I want happiness." We are all born with this as a basic part of our human nature. No religion has to teach us that, and no law has forced us to feel this way. It's not even necessary for a parent to teach us these feelings. It's instant, natural. I try to avoid any source of suffering and unhappiness. I try to find the aspects in life that bring me happiness, whether they're love or money or friends. And as long as people out there have this natural instinct like I do—wanting joy and avoiding hardship—then I should care for them. I should not try to hurt them because when people hurt me, I don't like it.

Now we're not really talking about religion here, right? We're talking about a natural thing; this is our reality.

In spite of all our differences, we are similar in that we all want to be happy; we don't want to suffer. That is enough to illustrate how alike we are at our core. We don't need any other reason to love others. It doesn't matter what religion they practice, what race they are, what kind of social condition they are in. It doesn't matter because we are all alike in this quintessential way. When we begin to truly see that this one similarity is what matters, then we can begin to love all beings. In Tibetan, we call that kind of great love *Jampa Chenpo, Nyingje Chenpo*, which means "great love and great compassion." The Dalai Lama often mentions that our focus and energy are so geared toward the intellectual side of our mind that we leave our heart's nurturing either to religious institutions or to our parents, but there is actually no dedicated time and space in our everyday lives to focus on this.

There is a big difference between knowing about love and compassion and embodying their qualities. Love and compassion are like plants. They start from a very simple seed and then gradually evolve. His Holiness the Dalai Lama says we have almost too much intelligence and a lack of heart. Because of that imbalance, we get into trouble because our intentions aren't as focused as they should be. We have incredible intelligence; therefore, we are capable of doing incredible things. It's unbelievable what we are able to do. But if intelligence is not accompanied by love and compassion, then it can become blind intelligence.

It can be destructive, too. We've witnessed destructive intelligence in our world when people focus on the advent of new ways to hurt others. But if it is accompanied by thoughtfulness and tolerance, that intelligence can become a very positive force. We have been evolving for millennia because we are a living phenomenon. It's the same with plants, animals, and all the different natural phenomena out there; when it is living, then it is natural to evolve. Plants evolve based on what kinds of causes and conditions affect it, just as many animal species have evolved. Humans have evolved and created cultures, art, literature, technologies, and so on, and it's amazing but natural that we've done so, because we nurture our intelligence. When we begin to concentrate more on these positive feelings—love, kindness, compassion— they can evolve if they are met with the right conditions, because they are also a natural phenomenon.

The Galapagos Island Finches

In 1836, when Charles Darwin returned to England after the HMS *Beagle*'s five-year journey, he identified thirteen different species of finches that had been collected, though he knew there was only one species of Finch on the South American mainland. By studying the different beak sizes and shapes, Darwin became the first person to discover adaptive radiation of a species.

Adaptive radiation happens when a species must acclimate to different ecological niches, eventually resulting in different species. The Galapagos finches all differed just slightly from each other, just as their environments did, thus giving each finch an advantage in staying alive and reproducing in its environment. These finches not only showed the way different conditions affect evolution, but they were also what helped Darwin come to the theory of natural selection.

❁ ❁ ❁

Like the finches, our human feelings can evolve when met with the right causes and conditions; they can evolve our heart.

They can become unconditional kindness. We can truly embody that quality, as the mother with her only child does, according to a thousand-year-old Tibetan legend. We can extend that love and compassion to all beings. Evolution is one of the natural laws, and knowing this, that we have the ability to change into compassionate beings, we can be more hopeful. We can see that maybe this really is possible for us all. When many of the great religions of the world describe their god, they talk about universal love. One of the great qualities of God is that She is all-loving. She is the supreme, the ultimate. Anyone who can be all-loving is the ultimate. In the Buddhist tradition, we say "enlightened being" instead of "god," but this pretty much means the same thing. Whenever we describe an enlightened being, that entity has universal love and compassion—what, in the Mahayana Tibetan Buddhist tradition, we call "bodhicitta." We try to cultivate that, to become it, and sometimes we can see that the possibility is there.

When we become more loving, more compassionate, and kinder, it does not mean that we have to be naïve or weak. This needs to be very clear. In truth, if we want to be loving people, compassionate people, kind people—not only loving a small circle of people but all beings, all humanity—then we have to be strong. We must be wise, not naïve. If we are not wise and strong, then people can take advantage of us. If we are strong, like Martin Luther King Jr., Mahatma Gandhi, or Aung San Suu Kyi—who has been under house arrest for more than a decade as punishment for her actions to implement democracy in Myanmar—then we realize that the lives and the happiness of the many are greater than those of the few. To make such personal sacrifices for the sake of humanity requires strength along with compassion.

Kindness Profile: Aung San Suu Kyi

After living in the United Kingdom and India, Aung San Suu Kyi (1945–) returned to Myanmar (known as Burma at the time) to nurse her sick mother and became involved in the pro-democracy movement of 1988. After returning to Rangoon, the capital of Burma, in April, Suu Kyi did not play a large part in the political uprising until violent military action killed thousands of people during mass democracy demonstrations on August 8 (known as 8-8-88). Suu Kyi's subsequent non-violent campaign for democracy has included letter writing, hunger strikes, and published books as well as the famous Irrawaddy Delta incident that is depicted in the 1995 film *O*.

On April 5, 1989, while touring the country speaking on democratic freedom and human rights, Suu Kyi was confronted by a military campaign in the Irrawaddy Delta in Rangoon, blocking a street where she and her supporters were walking. When the soldiers threatened to shoot, Suu Kyi walked up to them, requesting that her followers stay behind. She courageously approached these soldiers, staring down the barrels of numerous guns, because she knew they were looking for her and she did not want her followers to be caught in the line of fire. She later said, "It seemed so much simpler to provide them with a single target than to bring everyone else in."

In 1991 Suu Kyi was awarded the Nobel Peace Prize. In a press release, the Norwegian Nobel Committee stated that it "wishes to honor this woman for her unflagging efforts and to show its support for the many people throughout the world who are striving to attain democracy, human rights, and ethnic conciliation by peaceful means." In the face of violence, Suu Kyi has stayed true to her followers and peaceful to those threatening her, truly embodying strength and compassion.

◎ ◎ ◎

Suu Kyi's kind of fearless courage is true strength. Strength is fearlessness; when we believe in something, we're not afraid of doing it even at the cost of our life. That is real strength. We need to be strong in this way. We can be humble to people, but inside, we must be strong and wise. If we are not, people can fool us. Once we have this foundation of strength and wisdom, we can practice kindness effectively.

Cultivate these qualities inside you, and then implement them in your life. The more you become compassionate and caring, the more your responsibility to serve others grows to include not just yourself and your circle. As your responsibility becomes greater, naturally, you have to be wiser and stronger. You need mental strength; you need to have a mind that is fearless, courageous, and truly determined to do positive things. You will be determined, not afraid—that is the kind of strength you need. Mother Teresa and Mahatma Gandhi were not very strong physically; to look at them, especially near the end of their lives, they were simply a little old lady and a skinny old man, but their minds were strong, courageous, and determined.

Many people today think that universal kindness, compassion, and love don't work. They believe that these values are idealistic and impractical. This world is very tough, and too many people feel that they must be aggressive fighters, avengers. It's true; we do have to be tough. The difference between this fighter viewpoint and compassion is that we have to be staunch in our convictions, in our heart, and in our belief that true compassion is more effective than vengeance.

There can be truth in the thinking that compassion and kindness won't work and that people will take advantage of us, but if we are wise and strong, people will not be able to; they won't be able to fool us. By being strong and wise, this compassionate, kind, and loving way of life will succeed. This can work in the world. Mahatma Gandhi faced one of the world's superpowers, but he was wise and strong. Every day Mother Teresa could have contracted any number of illnesses from the people she was helping and nurturing on the street, but she was not afraid. She had an incredibly courageous, fearless heart.

An eye for an eye makes the whole world blind.
—**Mahatma Gandhi**

We also need to look at kindness as if it were a beautiful flower. To grow a flower, to help it blossom and live as long as it can, we need to constantly nurture it, starting from the time it is a seed, putting it in the soil, giving it water, heat, and air. When a seed slowly grows and becomes a beautiful flower, constant tending makes it blossom. The process is the same with our heart and soul: if we don't look after our heart, compassion won't suddenly manifest. Love and compassion will only grow inside our heart if we care for it. The seed is already there, always waiting for us to tap into it.

You have had a beautiful heart since before you were born; it's always been there, and it has always held the potential to love others. From childhood, some people are very kind and caring; some are quite disturbed, and it takes a long time for them to come around, but they also have all the capacity to become loving and compassionate. We need to always see that. If we reincarnate, the next life is a different story, but our current reality is in the here and now. If we can take care in this life, every day, then whatever we encounter in the future will take care of itself. If there is no such thing as the next life, then at the end of this life, we have no regrets because we have done our best and lived our best possible life. So we live quite happily because we are trying to live lives that are grounded in love, compassion, and kindness.

It is just a matter of trying—making an effort to tap into compassion—every day. If you can do that, then you can see results day by day, month by month, year by year, and if you believe in a next life, then in every life you'll get better and you'll realize your heart's full potential. Our heart has the seed of love, compassion, and kindness. It is there. No matter who you are, there is a seed of goodness; we Tibetans might say it is a seed of Buddha Nature.

You, no less than all beings, have Buddha Nature within.
—**Dhammavadaka**

Part of Buddha Nature is seeing the value in compassion and kindness. In this world, we value everything, but a lot of the time, we focus on the material or what can get us material things. We value education; we value money; we value our home; we value everything. But we don't value kindness and compassion enough. That's the problem. What makes something valuable or useless? The demarcation between what is valuable and what is not is if it brings comfort in life. Whatever helps reduce adversity is valuable.

Why is money valuable? Because we need clothes to keep us warm, shelter to protect us from the elements, and medicine and food to keep us healthy, and money can provide all those things. The uses and value of money go on and on. Why are friends valuable? Because, as the Dalai Lama says, human beings are social animals, so friends are a source of happiness. Why is a partner valuable? As traditional Western wedding vows say, we have someone, for richer or poorer, in sickness and in health. When we're sick or have a problem, then our partner is there for us. When we are happy and successful, we share the joy together. This is very valuable. When something brings joy and minimizes suffering, its value grows. Now think

41

about a smile, a kind word, or a surprise act of kindness from a friend or a stranger. What is the value of these things? They can all help with mental as well as physical well-being.

The Positive Effects of Kindness

While the list of things that are bad for us continues to grow, studies are continually exposing the positive health effects of kindness as well, so we can stay firm in the belief that kindness is truly beneficial to us all.

Kindness:

Increases our energy
Improves sleep patterns
Builds a stronger immune system
Assists with weight control
Increases body heat
Builds a healthier cardiovascular system
Reduces stomach acid
Decreases oxygen requirements
Helps relieve arthritis and asthma
Contributes to a speedier recovery from surgery
Reduces cancer activity
Produces serotonin, making us happier

◎　◎　◎

As Rabbi Harold Kushner pointed out, "When you carry out acts of kindness you get a wonderful feeling inside. It is as though something inside your body responds and says, yes, this is how I ought to feel." In this way, even being kind to yourself creates more happiness in your own life. When an act as simple as smiling or giving someone a kind word actually makes you happy, it has true value. This book is all about reintroducing ourselves to the value of kindness and compassion so that we can nurture these qualities within. The whole point is how kindness, love, and compassion are valuable. In this way, we are going back to the basics: these positive feelings can bring us happiness. Kindness and compassion are as important, if not more so, than all the material objects in the world. Look at all the particulars of life that we work so hard for—we cannot be happy and fully experience the material world without love and compassion, too. They are just as important.

Now imagine a president or a prime minister who truly values kindness and compassion; how much could that affect all the nations of the world? Imagine if all the wealthy people—billionaires and millionaires, Hollywood filmmakers, television network owners—were kinder; imagine how much of a difference that could make.

Once we begin to truly see the value in kindness and our own potential to feel universal bodhicitta, we can begin to work at feeling it. In Tibet, you can truly make yourself holy. If you really become a being who can feel universal love, kindness, and compassion, then you become a *bodhisattva*. If you can become the kind of being who can love all beings and place no conditions on that love, then you become holy.

The process does take time and effort, though. Khunu Lama Rinpoche, one of the Dalai Lama's teachers, compares it to the practice of some hermit meditators in Eastern Tibet. Some of these hermits meditate for ten to twelve years in the mountains, trying to cultivate universal love and compassion. Gradually, their hearts start to really open up and go past all the boundaries and conditions, and they are able to love all beings. This happens in two stages, the first with effort—what Tibetans call *tsolchey*. This requires meditating every day, contemplating every day, working on our heart every day, putting effort in. When we are concentrating on compassion, even for half an hour, we can begin to feel the difference it is making. It's like turning on a heater at home. Slowly, the house will start to heat up. Our heart can warm up in that way, with effort.

When we begin to feel this, it is a sign that a real transformation is taking place inside. After years of really working on their hearts, hermit meditators will begin to generate spontaneous universal love and compassion. Even the wild animals that live in the mountains become like domesticated animals in the presence of these meditators; they are totally fearless around the hermits. Animals have a good sense of kindness, and they feel it so strongly around these hermits who have achieved bodhicitta that they want to be around them more.

When we transform, those around us, whether they are animals or humans, can sense it. The more we become truly caring, the more everyone around will feel it, and they will benefit spontaneously. Everyone enjoys being around us when we become that kind of person. We can sometimes see this happen in our own families or groups of friends; people are drawn to the kindest people. It's because they feel so comfortable and safe. It feels truly comforting to be around that person who is very kind and caring and loving.

If we familiarize our mind and heart with kindness and patience, it will become second nature to us to be a very kind and patient person. This is the second stage, when we become so well trained and full of love and compassion that this state becomes second nature to us, effortless—we call this *tsolmay*. It can actually be compared to many skills we have to learn gradually, such as writing. It probably took you quite a while to be able to write an *a*, and now you can write it without thinking about the process. Professional athletes are a good example of this as well. For gymnasts, the movements and routines are difficult, and they have to practice hard every day. They have to train to make what they do look easy to the rest of us, and it looks effortless not because it doesn't take effort but because they trained so hard that it became second nature for them.

Compassion and kindness are not going to drop from the sky. The transformation takes place in tsolchey. We have to put consistent effort into it. The analogy of kindness as a plant that needs consistent nurturing is helpful here as well. If we do that, year by year, we get better and better. Right now, maybe you can kind of feel good about or close to a certain number of people. In a few years' time, your heart may become so open that you may feel the same goodness and closeness toward all human beings and hopefully other species who share this planet with us. You realize that seed of Buddha Nature, of true kindness, in your heart, and you water it every day, just as you would take care of any other living thing.

With meditation, we use our minds to cultivate and train ourselves to be more compassionate, more loving, and kinder. Meditation is a universal tool—in the Tibetan tradition we say *gom*, which means "familiarizing." In Tibet it is said, "*Gyomna Laawar, Migyur Wey, Nyoedey Gangyang Yoe Mayin*," which means, "Through familiarity, there is nothing that doesn't get easier." In meditation, we are familiarizing our mind with something, with a specific spiritual essence. If we familiarize our mind with peaceful breath, then we can gradually become peaceful. Personally, I really like meditating on compassion, kindness, and love. What can happen is, the more we familiarize our heart and mind with love, compassion, and kindness, these inner qualities gradually become our second nature.

In Tibetan tradition, we talk about how the mind has two aspects, *loong* and *sem*. Sem is clarity; this is awareness and being conscious of different phenomena. That is one of the functions of the mind. The other side is loong, which is when your active mind is aware of something—for example, when you hear a sound and your awareness suddenly moves to that sound. The energy that moves your awareness around, loong, aids in subtly moving your awareness throughout your body. These are the two qualities you want to be aware of as you meditate: the movement of your awareness and the awareness itself, the ability to be aware of the different phenomena. The awareness should be in different places at different times: on your breath, on the meditative phrase, and so on. When that awareness moves, be aware of its movement and where it has gone.

In the West, when people see a meditation tool, they usually think about single-pointed meditation. In the Tibetan tradition, we have two kinds of meditation. *Jog-Gom* means "single-pointed meditation," whether that point is your breath or a visualization of a divine being. Breathing meditation is also part of the yoga tradition. In India, it's a prominent part of the Hindu tradition and the Buddhist tradition. We call it *Loong Joong Nyoop Ki Gom*. It is utilized as one of the important tools in meditation.

The other type of meditation is *Chay-Gom*, which means "analytical meditation," and this uses the maximum intelligence of human beings. The more we use it, the sharper and more highly evolved we become. We have an incredible brain that we can analyze and reason with, so we can use this to truly focus on kindness, compassion, and love.

Analytical meditation is one of the most powerful tools we can use to transform human consciousness as well as our hearts and minds, especially to cultivate universal love and compassion. Therefore, of all the meditation tools, analytical meditation is one of the most treasured and is always encouraged by His Holiness the Dalai Lama. This method of meditation is like churning milk to make butter; we churn the milk of our human consciousness in order to manifest universal kindness and compassion. Of course, both analytical and single-pointed meditations are done on the basis of extensive study on the subject matter of the meditations; therefore, monks and nuns study for decades in the monasteries and nunneries, and even lay practitioners study extensively in their own ways.

Meditation Tool: Posture and Breathing Meditation

Before you begin meditating, think of your meditation posture. You can sit on a chair with back support or on the floor with a cushion or a mat, cross-legged. If you prefer, you can sit in the semi-lotus position, which is on the floor with each leg bent and each foot resting on the opposite leg's thigh. For this beginning meditation, a simple sitting posture is fine.

With all meditations, keep in mind:

- Sit up straight; have a straight spine
- Your back, neck, and shoulders should be relaxed
- Clear your mind so you can be aware and conscious of your meditation

Also be aware of what you are doing with your hands: left on bottom, right on top, both palms facing up and the tips of your thumbs touching. The thumbs should touch somewhere at the level of your navel. There are a few ways to hold your head, but try bending it slightly forward, but not so far that you become sleepy. Allow your eyes to semi-open and gaze out over the tip of your nose. This natural gaze can help you collect all your distracted thoughts into a completely focused state of mind. For a relaxing meditation like this one, you also can close your eyes. Your mouth and jaw should be relaxed and natural as well, so touch the tip of your tongue gently to your upper palate. Your mouth should just be closed naturally.

We all breathe, so this is one of the simplest as well as the most beneficial meditations to begin with. Breathe naturally, through your nose if possible or comfortable. Be aware of the sensation of your breath as it enters and leaves your nostrils. This sensation should be the single-pointed focus of your meditation when you first begin. Try to concentrate on it to the exclusion of everything else.

At first, your mind will be busy, and you might feel your awareness moving. If this happens, you may actually be improving your meditation practice, as you are becoming more aware of how your awareness moves. Try, in spite of feeling your awareness move around, to remain focused single-pointedly on the sensation of the breath. If you find that your awareness has wandered and is focusing on thoughts, surroundings, and so on, immediately but gently return your awareness to your breath. Repeat this whenever you can until your mind settles on your breath regularly.

Set aside some time every day to contemplate your breath, or even everyday wonders—the sun shining, the beauty we can find in simple objects—to truly benefit these positive human values in your heart. Then, slowly but steadily, you will truly become inspired by these inner values, and your heart will open. This is when your true humanity starts to take root within your heart and mind. The great master Khunu Lama Rinpoche said, "[Meditation] is how it is possible how an individual can transform his or her heart and become more loving, kind, and compassionate."

❁ ❁ ❁

After becoming familiar with the basic breathing meditation practice, begin meditating on this simple phrase: *May all be kind to each other.*

I created this phrase, and it is now endorsed and blessed by ten Nobel Peace Laureates: the Dalai Lama, Desmond Tutu, Betty Williams, Jody Williams, President José Ramos-Horta, Rigoberta Menchú Tum, President Óscar Arias Sánchez, Shirin Ebadi, Adolfo Pérez Esquivel, and Mairead Corrigan-Maguire.

Set aside time every day to meditate on kindness. Even ten minutes a day will help you begin to show an improvement. If you are particularly busy on a specific day, find a few minutes when you are alone and can relax, even if it is in the restroom, to concentrate on this phrase and the value of kindness. Later in the book, we will learn meditation tools that may fit into your busy life better, but this simple meditation is a beautiful place to start.

Tibetan Legend: Atisha

In Tibet, we have the great saint Atisha, who was born an Indian prince but then decided to become a monk. He studied intensively and meditated for years in solitude. Then, seventeen years before his death, he went to Tibet and lived there for the rest of his life. With all his extensive study, he was a very enlightened being, what we call *Drupchen*, which means that he achieved vast wisdom, and he saw kindness as one of the most important messages he could share. He was a great master, but his message was very simple. When he would meet people and they would greet him with, "Good morning," he would say, "Have you been kind?" When people departed, he would say, "Please try to be kind." That was his main message: kindness.

3

Awakening Your Own Kindness

If you want others to be happy, practice compassion.
If you want to be happy, practice compassion.

—His Holiness the Dalai Lama

The first person you must learn to be kind to is yourself. It is often difficult for us to fully accept that without being kind to ourselves, we are not equipped to be truly kind to others. We must take care of ourselves wisely, and the most effective and positive way to do this is living in kindness, love, and compassion. We know what these feelings are, what these words mean—to be nice and to care about others' well-being and suffering—but we don't always relate it directly to the simple ways we are kind to ourselves every day.

While contemplating basic human nature—that we all want happiness and none of us want to suffer—I can go through the details of my everyday routine and see how I take care of myself in little ways. When I wake up in the morning, I brush my teeth, then take a shower, put on nice clothes, have breakfast, and then go to work and do different things—try to earn some money, be with and make friends, have a nice house, and so on. All these different activities are things I do every day. If I ask myself why I do these things, the answer is always the same: I want to be happy, and I do not want to suffer or be sad.

If we don't brush our teeth, then our teeth become bad, and we will get cavities or toothaches or any number of other problems. Our teeth are some of our most useful equipment, not only for smiling but also for eating and talking. Where I once lived in India, there are people who live in the forest and don't use ordinary toothbrushes. They have a special, medicinal herb tree. They cut chewing sticks from it that become like toothbrushes. While the city dwellers and townspeople in India do it the "fancy" way we do here, with toothbrushes and store-bought toothpaste, the forest people do the same task in a different manner. Here is a clear example of doing things in different ways, but it shows that we all do what we do for the same reason: to take care of ourselves.

If we contemplate on this and go through all the different things that we do on a daily basis to take care of ourselves, we start to understand that our natural instincts are to take care of ourselves, and this is something we have in common with everyone else. From this, we can begin to see that our basic human instinct gives us a deep conviction to take care of ourselves, which is why we are doing all these things. Now take that conviction and look outside yourself.

All other people are doing similar things. They all get up in the morning, brush their teeth, take showers, try to have friends, earn some money, and so on. Why? They also want to take care of themselves. When you see that very clearly, then you can feel that fellow human beings are like you. This is when you begin to feel connected. Naturally, I say to myself, "I don't like when people hurt me, so I should not hurt other people. When people are kind and good to me, I truly appreciate it. Therefore, I should try my best to be kind and serving to other people." This, at its core, is a decision to be kind to ourselves, as we are showing to the world and ourselves how we want to be treated: kindly.

This is also when our hearts start to open. This simple realization, that being kind to others is simply an illustration of how we want others to treat us, is our first tool; it is common sense but very profound. It's universal. We don't have to be Buddhist for this; in fact, it is a main tenet of all great religions:

Christianity—All things whatsoever ye would that men should do to you, do ye so to them; for this is the law and the prophets. (Matthew 7:12)

Confucianism—Do not do to others what you would not like yourself. Then there will be no resentment against you, either in the family or in the state. (Analects 12:2)

Buddhism—Hurt not others in ways that you yourself would find hurtful. (Udana-Varga 5,18)

Hinduism—This is the sum of duty; do naught onto others what you would not have them do unto you. (Mahabharata 5,1517)

Islam—No one of you is a believer until he desires for his brother that which he desires for himself. (40 Hadith of an-Nawawi 13)

Judaism—What is hateful to you, do not do to your fellowman. This is the entire Law; all the rest is commentary. (Talmud, Shabbat 3id)

Taoism—Regard your neighbor's gain as your gain, and your neighbor's loss as your own loss. (Tai Shang Kan Yin P'ien)

Wiccan—Whatever you send out, to you comes back times three. (The Three-fold Law)

Religion is actually a way that we take care of ourselves. Why are we drawn to religion? It is the ultimate source of protection for its followers. All the different religious traditions bring inspiration and spiritual help to us. People are drawn to religion. If we didn't care about our own happiness and sense of well-being, we wouldn't be so interested in religion. This all boils down to basic human nature: we want to be happy and to know that someone cares for us. It is all the more amazing when we realize that the kindness our religion asks us to practice is so universal, it can be found in all the great religions of the world.

It starts to become clear that taking care of ourselves is also a kindness to others. A good way to understand this is to think about the flight attendant's instructions when you're traveling on a plane: if the plane loses cabin pressure, even if you are traveling with someone, you should secure your own oxygen mask first. This is because if you try to keep others safe before yourself, neither of you will be safe. In the same way, you have to show kindness to yourself and take care of yourself before you're equipped to do so for others.

It is imperative that we learn to nurture and be kind to ourselves. Just as kindness affects our well-being, so does its opposite: anger, both when it is directed at ourselves and when it is directed at others. Our anger makes us unhappy first and foremost. No one ever says, "I was really angry, so I had a great time today." Usually, when we are angry, it affects us physically as well. Anger causes high blood pressure, headaches, and other health issues. We destroy our physical balance with anger. When we show anger, we also expose a dark, unattractive side of our being. But if we can go beyond anger, we can become peaceful, patient, and beautiful.

⊙ ⊙ ⊙ ⊙ ⊙ ⊙ ⊙ ⊙ ⊙

Health Risks of Anger

Many recent studies, including the study "Anger and Health" by Steven Stosny, PhD, have found that anger contributes to a number of health issues, including but not limited to:

- High blood pressure, which in turn contributes to a higher risk of heart disease
- Headaches
- Weight gain
- Increased risk of depression
- Digestion problems
- Insomnia
- Skin problems

- Strokes
- Breathing problems

These are just a few of the problems listed from only a handful of studies concerning the adverse effects of anger on physical health. There are also many proposed solutions to combat anger, which include incorporating an exercise regimen, keeping a diary, and practicing yoga or meditation. The emotional advice most often listed is to accept that anger is a natural emotion that can actually be healthy when handled appropriately.

o o o o o o o o o

When we are frustrated and angry, we might do things we don't normally do. Anger transforms our actions negatively, but there is a way to transform your anger. Rather than suppressing it, we can transform it through wisdom. This is one of the best gifts we can give ourselves. If we are less angry, less suffering—our own and others'—is created from our anger. With our free will, we can realize, "If I have a choice, I should be less angry." Even just that mere understanding helps us be calmer. In the same way that heat and light make ice melt into water, this simple wisdom transforms our anger into kindness. A lot of things depend on intention and how we motivate ourselves. If we intend to be less angry and more patient, this intention is good for us; it is good for everybody.

In the eighth century, the great Indian master Shantideva composed a phrase that has become a favorite of the Dalai Lama's. The great saint said, "*Geltey Choe-soo Yoe-nani, Dela Migar Jaychi Yoe, Geltey Choe-soo Mey-nani, Dela Migar Jaychi Feyn.*" This translates loosely to "If there is a way or a solution to the problem, what is there to be worried and upset about? If there is no way or solution to the problem, what is the use of being upset about it?" When you think that way, it helps expose the futility of anger and frustration. Everything boils down to these two points. If there is already a problem—whether it's a physical problem like a broken leg or a life circumstance such as the weather—the question becomes, Can I change it, and if so, how? Perhaps you can change it, which means that soon there will be nothing to be angry over. If there is no solution and you have to live with it, there is no point in being upset; you simply have to accept it.

There is a very funny story in Tibet, a classic tale that tells of two friends. One of them had learned how to meditate. The meditating friend was sitting and practicing, and his friend came by and asked, "What are you doing here?"

And he said, "I'm meditating on patience."

His friend said, "Oh, come on. Bullshit."

"What did you just say?" the meditator friend asked, clearly bothered.

"Didn't you say you were meditating on patience?" his friend said. "You shouldn't be so upset then."

This story is funny to consider because the friend is actually helping the meditator put his patience into action. You can meditate on patience, but it is very hard.

We say that cultivating patience is similar to training to be a good boxer: You need a good opponent to train with. If your opponent is the easiest person and you win without a challenge, you will not be a good boxer. You need to have a good opponent who will give you a few good blows so that you can learn effective defense as well as offense. The more you practice with a good opponent, the better the boxer you become.

Every morning, the Dalai Lama's recites the spiritual poetry of the "Eight Verses for Training the Mind," one of which says:

Gangla Dakgi Fen-takpa, Reywa Cheywa Gang-shik Gi, Shintoo Mirik Noe Jeyna Yang, Shey Nyen Damper Tawar Shok.

In English, this translates to:

When someone whom I have helped,

Or in whom I have placed great hopes,
Mistreats me in extremely hurtful ways,
May I regard him still as my precious teacher.

We must consider those who challenge us and those who hurt us as our mentors because they teach us patience. Anger is the biggest hindrance to love and compassion, but when we put forth the intention to learn from it, we let go of anger and step fully into kindness.

The Eight Verses for Training the Mind

by Geshe Langri Thangpa (translation from His Holiness the Dalai Lama's website, www.dalailama.com).

With a determination to achieve the highest aim
For the benefit of all sentient beings
Which surpasses even the wish-fulfilling gem,
May I hold them dear at all times.

Whenever I interact with someone,
May I view myself as the lowest amongst all,
And, from the very depths of my heart,
Respectfully hold others as superior.

In all my deeds may I probe into my mind,
And as soon as mental and emotional afflictions arise—
As they endanger myself and others—
May I strongly confront them and avert them.

When I see beings of unpleasant character
Oppressed by strong negativity and suffering,
May I hold them dear—for they are rare to find—
As if I have discovered a jewel treasure!

When others, out of jealousy,
Treat me wrongly with abuse, slander, and scorn,
May I take upon myself the defeat
And offer to others the victory.

When someone whom I have helped,
Or in whom I have placed great hopes,
Mistreats me in extremely hurtful ways,
May I regard him still as my precious teacher.

In brief, may I offer benefit and joy
To all my mothers, both directly and indirectly,
May I quietly take upon myself
All hurts and pains of my mothers.

May all this remain undefiled
By the stains of the eight mundane concerns;
And may I, recognizing all things as illusion,
Devoid of clinging, be released from bondage.

The ultimate solution to anger is to become a more patient human being, to go beyond anger. That is the key to resolving frustration. That is how to transform our frustration. At the same time, it is important to understand that, as human beings, we naturally become frustrated. It's part of who we are. We can't be too hard on ourselves when we get frustrated, especially when we are upset for good cause, but we do want to transform our frustration, hopefully before it evolves into anger.

I have found that the Buddhist tradition has certain mindful practices, especially in the Theravada Buddhist tradition, that are helpful for transforming anger. Theravada Buddhists do a special mindful meditation that is wonderful. When you are getting angry—when you feel the heat and sensation of anger in your body—instead of mindlessly letting it overwhelm you, just focus your mind on that feeling. Focus on the sensation of the anger in your head, your body. Just feel it. Focus on that completely, and take that like the alarm saying, "You're getting angry. Wake up." If you focus your mind on that sensation of anger, gradually you start to calm down; it's like boiling water when you pour cold water into it. That cool water of mindfulness calms that boiling anger. When you are calmer, then you can focus on constructive ways to solve the problem if it is solvable.

Frustration is like the darkness in a room. As the light hits the room more, the darkness will be transformed into light. Wisdom is the light; the more wisdom we can gather, the more it will help transform our frustration. When you start getting frustrated, you can meditate on the sensation of frustration and even envision your wisdom lighting that darkness. It can really help calm your frustration.

Nonviolence is a powerful and just weapon,
which cuts without wounding and ennobles the man
who wields it. It is a sword that heals.
        —Martin Luther King Jr.

By getting out of a more wrathful space, we can figure out how to deal with problems in a nonviolent way. It's very important to approach problems in a nonviolent way and to remember that anger itself is a form of violence—inner violence. It doesn't help anybody. It brings us down and destroys our strength. The more unhappy and angry we become with the problems we see in the world—which include the Tibetan problem for me—the more it destroys our strength, which means that we become weaker. Just as the Dalai Lama has stayed strong and hopeful and has tried to solve the Tibetan problem—instead of simply being angry and speaking about revenge or punishment—we also want to find every possible way we can stay strong and consider how to solve any problem we encounter. If we do that, then we are not unhappy; we are doing our best to use our wisdom to stay calm and compassionate.

When faced with any problem, the first thing to do is say, "Relax," and then say, "Okay, what can I do to transform this problem?" There are always ways other than anger or violence. Sometimes the problem is so great and so immediate that we feel overwhelmed. As human beings, that's very natural, but we shouldn't be hard on ourselves if that is our initial response. Anger is a slippery slope, and if we get angry at first, we don't want to make it worse by directing anger at ourselves for having that response. After getting upset for a few hours, if we notice the emotion and build the intention to transform it, we can contemplate on wisdom and try to transcend that anger.

The Dalai Lama has said that when we are not angry, our mind is better equipped to calculate and do precisely what is necessary to take care of the situation. If we're angry, we might do something that makes the problem worse.

I would like to make a very important suggestion that when you first wake up in the morning, before you even open your eyes, just say to yourself, "Today I will try my best not to hurt any beings. I will try my best with my actions, with my words, and with my thoughts. I will try my best not to hurt anyone."

Thoughts, even though we can't directly see them, can also be violence. They are a subtle violence. Among all the different types of violence, that is the most primal kind. It starts in our own minds and hearts and is then expressed through verbal or physical means. Though we don't normally consider initial thoughts as actions, they are the seed of intent and action, so try to make this affirmation in the morning. In addition to that, you can also say, "I will try to be kind, compassionate, and helpful to anyone I encounter in these twenty-four hours."

Then, in the evening, before you go to sleep, the last thing you should do is examine your thoughts and actions. Ask yourself, "Have I lived according to my affirmation and not hurt any sentient beings? Have I tried to be kind and helpful?" I suggest that you buy a notebook and every day make a note regarding your actions and your kindness. In a few weeks you can check it to see if you have improved.

By embracing all these things, we begin to do everything we can. In that way, our journey on this road to compassion will become more successful. The bodhisattvas say, "Out of compassion you remain in the suffering world, but out of wisdom you stay out of the suffering." It's like swimming to rescue someone. If you are in the water and you know how to swim, you don't drown with her; you are there to minimize her suffering.

Only a life lived for others is a life worthwhile.
—**Albert Einstein**

Individualism and Bodhicitta

Individualism is often confused with being an individual in Western society. Being an individual, as in standing out from the crowd, is wonderful if that is how you like to live your life. The issue is when being an individual turns into individualism, which actually means that someone is focusing too much on just his or her own problems. This is the me-first culture of focusing all our energy only on ourselves. It becomes too self-centered and selfish. Slowly, though, individualism can be transformed. Like frustration or anger, it simply needs to be channeled properly.

Individualism is like a river. Not channeled properly, the river can cause floods. In society, when we become too self-centered, our demands flood the world with frustration, creating massive destruction. However, as I have said here, caring about ourselves is not selfish. If the river is channeled properly, it maintains an effective level of water to keep its current and to contribute to field irrigation and the town's drinking water. Likewise, you can easily first nurture yourself and still have concern for other beings. Sometimes the Dalai Lama says, "If you want to be selfish, then be wisely selfish. If you love others, then you will be the one who most benefits." That is bodhicitta.

Bodhicitta is actually very similar to individualism when it is founded on love and compassion. The foundation of bodhicitta says, "May I become fully enlightened in order to serve all sentient beings." That has two sides. The first part—may I become fully enlightened—shows that we are taking care of ourselves in the fullest way. When we become fully enlightened in the Buddhist idea, there is nothing greater that we can achieve. When we become fully enlightened, we become omniscient—all powerful and all loving. We have the seed of all these qualities within us. That means, then, that when we are omniscient and universally compassionate, we have the power of every ability. This also means that we become the greatest tool to serve others because we see everybody's need and are not selfish.

At the same time, you have the power to manifest that need. It's like the greatest individualism. You are taking care of yourself in the highest possible way, but bodhicitta is grounded in serving others. So it's a twofold achievement, and we can all try to accomplish it. I simply offer bodhicitta as an example for you, but the point is to take care of ourselves in the highest possible way and then to think about how to serve others. The idea is to truly try to cultivate universal love and compassion as much as we can in our life while realizing that when we achieve that cultivation, we truly benefit and become happier.

The best way to find yourself is to lose yourself
in the service of others.
—Mahatma Gandhi

Recently, a friend told me that when she is kinder and more caring, the first person to benefit is herself. She said that her day is immediately better. When we are really kind and loving to others, we are much happier. Kindness makes our day better because when we are kind and loving, wherever we go in this world, we will always find real friends. On the basis of that, if we are kind and compassionate, we will be very rich with friends. There's a proverb that says, "They are rich who have true friends." This does not just mean many friends, but it means genuine friends who truly care about others, who care about who we are inside and not about how much money or beauty or power we have. The friends who come and go when we lose these things are not true friends. But people who love us because we have a true, good heart—these friends are valuable and will stay with us the rest of our life. In that, our kindness will bring us riches.

Friends can be an important part of finding meaning in our life. We all seek meaning, and we can feel empty when we can't find it. But if we can be truly loving, compassionate, and kind, hopefully to all beings, then we have found our life's purpose. The highest meaning in life is to serve all other beings. Our true aim, as Saint Francis would say, is to become an instrument for peace. If you believe in God, then you become a servant of God. In Buddhism, this is when you become an enlightened being, which we describe as having three qualities: ability, wisdom, and universal compassion and love for all beings. If there's any job enlightened beings have, it is to care about other beings. And if we are doing that—dedicating our life to serving others—then we truly become enlightened, and then we truly become a servant of God, an attendant to humanity.

We make a living by what we get,
but we make a life by what we give.
—Winston Churchill

When we are good-hearted, we are immediately relieved of a lot of our inner turmoil and dissatisfaction. We know that whenever we feel love toward others, it does something to us. There is a reason that so many people look for love in all its forms: it brings true happiness.

Meditation Tool: Day of Kindness

The idea of adopting a day of kindness is like eating a delicious ice cream: once you've tried it, you truly know the delightfulness of the treat. In the same way, if you can experience the wonders, beauty, and meaningfulness of receiving kindness, you may want to be kinder throughout your life. Therefore it could be beautiful to try to practice a Day of Kindness.

From this moment through the next twenty-four hours, adopt a Day of Kindness. The idea for a Day of Kindness is to spend at least one day out of the year really celebrating and focusing on kindness—just as we celebrate different people every year on, for instance, Father's Day or Mother's Day. You can adopt this day at any time, so I suggest making the next twenty-four hours your Day of Kindness. During this day, really try to turn your heart and mind to kindness. Here are some tactics to help you:

- When you're talking to people, ask yourself, "Am I speaking kindly?"
- When you're walking, ask yourself, "Am I walking kindly?"
- When you are doing anything, ask yourself, "Am I doing this kindly?"

This is what bodhisattvas do; they really tune their whole being and all their actions toward not hurting anyone and always trying to benefit others through kindness and servitude.

While you are eating, think about the kindness of all the beings that were involved in making your food: the four elements, the farmers who worked so hard on cultivating the food, the people who cooked it, and the animals that also lived off the land and/or fertilized it. Think about how much hard work all the beings did and how much care they gave so you could have the food you are eating, and be grateful and say thank you for that. Think about how you've been given a place to sit and this book to read. Many people have worked hard to create the place where you are sitting and this book you are reading, so try to think about that and say thank you. Behind everything, there has been so much hard work, so reflect for an entire day on the kindness of others that has brought you to where you are.

You can also think about or try to engage in these simple kindness practices during the Day of Kindness:

- Try to patch up a strained relationship. Maybe you haven't spoken to a person for years due to some silly mistake or misunderstanding. Send a simple gift with a note or call and say, "I miss you. Please forgive me." You never know what wonders a few kind words can do.
- Share a dollar or two with a homeless person.
- Give a kind smile to a sad and suffering person.
- Become a member of PETA or Amnesty International.
- Write a poem about kindness or think about writing a book or screenplay with a theme focused on love, kindness, compassion, and humor.
- Compose a song about love and compassion.
- If you are a parent or teacher, tell your children or students stories about kindness once a month.
- Make dinner at home for a week instead of going out to eat at a fast-food establishment or restaurant. Donate the money you save to a needy or worthy organization. Eating at home can also be good for your health.

Three Processes of Meditation

In meditation, we have three processes. The first is learning through study and the second process is finding deep conviction through contemplation of what was learned. Finally after learning and finding deep conviction, you go through the third process of meditating on it, cultivating it, and making a habit of it. Tibetan tradition calls this *Thoe Sam Gom Soom*: the three processes of learning, contemplating, and meditating.

Through listening—to CDs guiding meditation, in workshops or to teachings from great teachers, or even through reading books on meditation—we learn about cultivating kindness, love, and compassion. In the beginning, we can use tools like CDs to guide us. It's helpful to use these tools as we're learning to meditate, but at a certain point, it's important to meditate without them. Part of what the hermits do is sit and contemplate on their own.

Through listening, you learn, but in the second part of the process, you take it one step further. You use the maximum power of your intelligence—your brain power—and then analyze what you've learned and think it through. Clarify it. Really see if it makes sense or not. You develop a deep sense of awareness. You have an insight about its meaning and value in your life, rather than just accepting a point on blind faith because it is in a book or an expert said it. Instead, you are really using your maximum intelligence to analyze it, either agreeing with it or adding to it or disputing it. When you do this, whatever you have learned becomes clear.

Through deep conviction, what you have learned becomes unshakably your own. At that point, if I were to say to you, "All I've said is wrong. Don't believe it," and you responded, "No, no, no. This is right because of this, this, and this," that would be because you have a deep conviction in it. For instance, a thousand people could come to me and say that hurting others is good and being kind and compassionate and serving others is bad, but it wouldn't matter. A thousand people cannot change my mind because, since I was inspired with kindness, I have lived through it and I have a deep conviction inside me that this is one of the greatest principles of life.

It's very important to have a deep conviction. Once you have that, no one can shake you up and change you. That's why in the Tibetan monasteries, the monks debate for hours and hours on one single point. They don't only debate with one person, they debate with thousands of people for years because they all have deep convictions about what they believe.

Traditional Tibetan Debate

While it is common in Western debate for the purpose to be winning, Tibetan debate is about expanding your mind, increasing mental sharpness, and gaining internal clarity. The defender presents his or her opinion, and the questioner raises doubts and points out weaknesses in the argument. Normally, a more experienced debater questions a novice monk (defender). By doing this, the defender learns to truly stand behind his or her opinions, even in the face of someone more experienced, someone acknowledged to have more wisdom. Traditionally, these types of training debates have a time limit (often two and a half hours), though debates among monks are a common part of daily monastery life, through which even the most experienced monks continue to expand their minds and gain spiritual experience.

Finally the whole point of learning and finding deep conviction for wisdom, love, kindness, and compassion is to embody these human values within, and to gradually become a wise, kind, compassionate, and loving person. For this to happen—whether you choose to live in a city around others or in solitude—you basically try your best to cultivate and make a habit of it, and then meditate on those inner values you have learned and find deep conviction for the rest of your life. Through this you become a better human being over the years.

Meditation Tool: Walking Kindness

The Walking Kindness Meditation is inspired by traditional Theravada and Vietnamese Buddhist walking meditation. You will use the same phrase as in the Breathing Meditation: "May all be kind to each other." Whenever you have time, you can do the Walking Kindness Meditation in your park or in nature or even just when you have the time to go for a quick walk around your block. The famous Buddhist monk Thich Nhat Hanh has made walking meditation very popular.

Walking meditation is a more mindful meditation than one that involves simply breathing, but it is what inspired me to create this new exercise. This tool is very useful because most people walk, so we can fit walking kindness meditation into our everyday lives. Walking from the car into a mall, to a bus stop, through a parking lot—walking just about anywhere can be an opportunity for a walking kindness meditation.

Walking itself can transform the way that we find peace, the way we find kindness and compassion and

nurture our hearts. Practicing the walking kindness meditation is part of my workshop. If you can, go somewhere
in nature where you don't have to be mindful of traffic and
where you can see a beautiful view. When you are walking, just walk very gently. You can also chant "May all be
kind to each other" in the process of walking, either aloud
or in your head. Now you can also walk silently while
focusing your mind and hearing on your walk, thinking of
kindness and compassion.

There are a few key differences between walking kindness
meditation and sitting meditation. Obviously, you want to
keep your eyes open during walking kindness meditation.
This change means there will be other alterations in the way
you do the practice. You do not want to draw your consciousness inward in the same way that you do when you practice
the Posture and Breathing Meditation outlined earlier. For
your safety, you have to be aware of the world outside yourself,
obviously, so you don't want to walk with your eyes closed.
Also, be aware of your other surroundings—the weather,
nature, sounds, and so on—and respond to them accordingly.
One very positive difference between walking kindness meditation and sitting meditation is that most people find it easier
to be aware of their bodies when they are in motion, so walking kindness meditation can be a very intense experience.

*People usually consider walking on water or in thin air
a miracle. But I think the real miracle is not to walk
either on water or in thin air, but to walk on earth.
Every day we are engaged in a miracle which we don't
even recognize: a blue sky, white clouds, green leaves,
the black, curious eyes of a child—our own two eyes.
All is a miracle.*

—**Thich Nhat Hanh**

4

Awakening Kindness with Others

All the kindness which a man puts out into the world
works on the heart and thoughts of mankind.

—Albert Schweitzer

Because of so many different people's kindness, we are able to achieve great things and even find happiness. Unfortunately, we often forget this and don't spend enough time reflecting on others' kindness and how we benefit from it. We are constantly nurtured by each other's kindness. As I mentioned earlier, it's actually easy to begin to truly appreciate the kindness of others if we think about something as simple as the food and drink that is digesting in our stomach right now, giving us energy and health. So many people were involved in the making of those things.

Even more simply, we can just think about the air we breathe. This planet didn't always have a breathable atmosphere, but after millennia of planetary change and plant life evolution, oxygen fills our atmosphere. If oxygen stops being produced, we will no longer be able to breathe. Thinking like that, we can be thankful to the air for every moment we are breathing and for the life it gives us. We can be thankful for all the organisms that have contributed to this. We can even be thankful for the water, the heat, everything; the more we can reflect on the interdependent nature of life—how much we are dependent on others—the more humble and grateful we are. Beginning there, we start to fully appreciate how much our treatment of others impacts our own lives, including the environment, our neighbors, and all species that live on this planet together.

It is very important to try to reflect every day on the interdependent nature of life and the kindness of others. Reflect on the four elements and on other sentient beings, human or non-human. It nurtures the heart. As I have mentioned, I am not an enlightened being, nor can I make anyone enlightened. I am the same kind of human being that you are, and the only thing we can do is take each day and try to spend it in a space of kindness. Try to feel kindness, compassion, and love. Most people who are reading this book are like-minded and admire kindness, compassion, and love. The fact that you are reading it shows you want to nurture this part of your most beautiful human quality.

Einstein was one of the greatest minds of the twentieth century, and had his guiding principles not been focused on kindness, compassion, and love, the world might now be a more dangerous place, as he could have used his amazing mind for more destructive endeavors. Like Einstein, if we let these principles guide our lives, we can see the difference our intentions make in the world. Kindness is also like art. It can transform who we are. It has the power to transform an ordinary being into an extraordinary being, just like art. For example, through art, Michelangelo was able to make one of the most incredible statues in the world: *David*. Because of art and its ability to transform, that ordinary stone was made into an extraordinary form of inspiration. This is what art and kindness can do: transform and inspire.

> *The ideals which have lighted my way, and time after time have given me new courage to face life cheerfully, have been Kindness, Beauty, and Truth.*
> **—Albert Einstein**

By being warmhearted, caring, and compassionate, you look beautiful. Even when you have physical beauty, if you have inner beauty as well, then no one can top that. A lot of older people I've seen, especially in Asia, have aged with a lot of wrinkles, but they are beautiful. They look like gorgeous pieces of art. While most cultures do not consider wrinkles a source of beauty, these people are very beautiful with their wrinkles. And the only reason that they could look so pleasing is because they have been kind throughout their lives. They always give very kind smiles to other people, and their joy is reflected in the wrinkles that all those smiles have caused.

This can be seen in myriad ways, too. When I lived in south India, I had a great Italian friend who was very kind-natured and had quite crooked teeth, but his smile was so incredibly broad that it didn't matter how his teeth looked. His face was so bright and joyful that every time I saw him, it made me so happy because the beauty in his heart was reflected in that smile.

There are many things in life that make us see how kindness, love, and compassion can transform individuals and truly bring peace and happiness—more than what money can provide. Money is important, of course; we need to pay our bills, we need to eat food, we need shelter from the elements. We do need money, but it is not the answer to everything. True joy and kindheartedness provide purer beauty and happiness than we could ever buy.

Mark Twain once said, "Age is an issue of mind over matter. If you don't mind it, it doesn't matter." This is interesting to contemplate when people worry about their wrinkles or when they feel like they look older. For the truly kind at heart, those who maintain inner beauty, that is what shines through. When you look at age in that way, then your perception of it and beauty can change.

In modern culture, there is a tendency to feel pressured to be perfect—to be the most successful, to have the best job or home, to look the youngest. Once when I was in Australia, I conducted a workshop with a tennis player who was playing in the Australian Open. He taught me a lot, and I began to understand the pressure in the West to allow no room for error, and why people feel a constant nagging to be the winner—literally or figuratively—and to be perfect. When we are kind and sweet to others, we are perfecting ourselves for our own good and for the good of humanity. We are simply going through the process of becoming a better human being, so we are not competing with anybody. By focusing on kindness, we go through a process to improve ourselves instead of feeling pressure to be perfect; we simply try our best. I found out from this tennis player that because of the pressure, we suffer a lot of damage when we don't succeed—and sometimes even when we do. Let go of the pressure. Then you can try all the possibilities, learn all the tools you can to make yourself the best person possible, and stop worrying about being perfect. Just do all the right exercises, concentrate, and learn.

Beyond that pressure to achieve perfection in success, we spend thousands of dollars on expensive clothes, accessories, and makeup to look perfect. Some people even spend thousands on face-lifts and plastic surgery. We spend so much money on our outward appearance because we feel pressured to look a certain way. These days we have Botox and all kinds of other chemicals that we pay people to inject into our bodies to rid ourselves of wrinkles. We do truly dangerous things—risking our long-term health—and spend so much money to make ourselves beautiful, but if we can realize and appreciate our inner values and focus on kindness, then we can naturally become beautiful for the reminder of our lives.

The Importance We Place on Outward Appearances

The American Society for Aesthetic Plastic Surgery (ASAPS) has reported more than ten million cosmetic procedures performed in the United States every year for the past three years. The ASAPS also reported that Americans spent more than $11 billion on cosmetic surgery in 2008 alone. This number doesn't include money spent on regular cosmetics, diet programs and foods, or quick-fix pills and gadgets. Just as with any surgical procedure, the risks involved in these practices include abnormal heart rhythm, blood clots, brain damage, heart attacks, nerve damage, strokes, temporary paralysis, and death. And yet many continue to take these risks to appeal to society's image of what is beautiful.

Regular cosmetics account for around $8 billion in annual revenue in the United States as we try to improve our outward appearances. An amazing number of Americans are willing to risk their lives to get plastic surgery, spend their savings on Botox, or invest in high-end makeup, designer clothes, gym memberships, and so on. If we all took the conviction that we have to appeal to others outwardly and channeled it into smiling, helping out, or simply giving a kind word to even one person every day, we would become more beautiful by leaps and bounds . . . and for free.

It is every human being's birthright to be beautiful; we *should* be beautiful, of course. This is our right, but one of the secrets to truly making ourselves beautiful inside and out is becoming a good, kindhearted person and truly caring for others. If this is the type of person you are, wherever you go, whomever you meet, whatever way you communicate with others—whatever it is you're doing—everything becomes beautiful.

For attractive lips, speak words of kindness.
For lovely eyes, seek out the good in people.
For a slim figure, share your food with the hungry.
For beautiful hair, let a child run his or her fingers
through it once a day.
For poise, walk with the knowledge that you never walk alone. . . .
People, even more than things, have to be restored, renewed,
revived, reclaimed and redeemed; never throw out anyone.
Remember, if you ever need a helping hand, you'll find one
at the end of each of your arms. As you grow older, you will
discover that you have two hands, one for helping yourself,
the other for helping others.

—Audrey Hepburn

Kindness creates beauty, and it also transcends all differences. I find the Dalai Lama a perfect example of this. He is different from many of his followers. First, he is Asian. Second, he is a monk, which means his appearance is different from that of most modern people, with a shaved head and monk's robes. But wherever he goes in this world, he transcends those differences. People are instantly drawn to him and love him. Why? Mainly, people want to be around him because of his heart. He truly has a compassionate, loving, warm heart, and that is the kind of inner beauty that transcends all these differences.

We also become more aware of beauty when we have a truly beautiful heart. We transform; we naturally become beautiful. Suddenly, we find beauty in ourselves and everyone else. We also find fairness, because when we are kind, we are fair. Unfairness comes from an unkind heart, but when we are at ease, we no longer feel as if we are in competition with other people, so we are calm. Humor comes naturally, too. The people out there who are great and enlightened have a lot of humor, because humor is similar to the openness of the heart. When we are kind, our heart is open, and we become at ease. When we are at ease, humor comes naturally.

A Nun's Sense of Humor

Mother Teresa was not well known for her sense of humor while she was alive. Instead, she was revered for her charity, her service to others, and her faith in God and the good in people. All great beings have a wonderful sense of humor, and this can be seen in Mother Teresa's life, even as she was facing death.

After becoming very ill with fever, she spoke of a dream she had in which she died and was sent to heaven. "I dreamed that I was at the gates of heaven. And Saint Peter said, 'Go back to Earth; there are no slums up here.'" She related the fact that she got very angry in her dream when he said this to her, responding, "Fine! Then I'll fill heaven with slum people, and you will have slums then!"

This anecdote, while of course being humorous, also clearly illustrates Mother Teresa's devotion to taking care of those who are least thought of. While many would not think that there are slums in heaven because it is heaven, Mother Teresa took what she dreamed as a sign that she should continue working for her cause—and continue it with the same temperament and ease that she always had.

As illustrated by Mother Teresa's humor, when we feel at ease, we have less fear and find it easier to have levity in certain situations. We have an unshakable and quiet confidence, and taking things lightly won't bother us—whether we are the ones taking matters lightly or others are. We can see this quiet confidence in Gandhi as well as in Mother Teresa. Even when they were faced with completely unfamiliar scenarios, they were filled with unshakable self-worth and confidence.

Wisdom is also very important, because many people look kind but don't really care about others' well-being. Those who don't care about others' suffering, happiness, or well-being just put on a pretty face and use flowery words to try to trick people. Sometimes people try to deceive us, and they use kindness or beauty as bait.

I heard a story once of a great yogi who was traveling, and he came upon a person pretending to be a beggar. The yogi stopped and tried to help this person, and the "beggar" tricked the yogi, took advantage of his kindness, and robbed him. This hurt the yogi deeply because he felt that that sort of deceptive and manipulative action can make people unappreciative of true generosity or uncomfortable with being generous. He was very saddened by that. We must remember that there are people who do these kinds of things. This is one reason why it's important to be wise and strong when being kind to others.

Wise and Strong

English nurse Florence Nightingale studied for years in many different hospitals in different countries before she went into the field of nursing. During the Crimean War, she stood her ground, arguing with those in charge of the hospital that patients' conditions were not sanitary enough. Eventually, her persistence paid off when sanitation specialists visited the hospital to help institute her proposed changes and the death rate fell.

Martin Luther King Jr. was faced with death threats, bombings, jail time, and physical violence during his many nonviolent campaigns. While he demonstrated his strength in acting out his campaigns, he also displayed his wisdom when he canceled marches because he felt the tension was too high and violence would happen. During the many acts of civil disobedience that King arranged and took part in, he was consistently strong and wise.

Mahatma Gandhi is often thought of as a man in robes, and though it is a well-known fact, not everyone remembers that Gandhi studied law at University College London and was a practicing lawyer. While still in London, Gandhi read the *Bhagavad Gita* and began studying Hindu and Christian texts. This background is what provided him with a solid knowledge and strong conviction in the political stances he took.

◎　◎　◎

Real kindness is present in these people as well as myriad others who have braved violence, illness, poverty, and judgment to stand up for others. This includes more than just the leaders of these well-known global movements and charities, too. Their followers—as well as people who show smaller kindnesses every day—should be admired; this type of altruism is real. The way Mother Teresa served her whole life and gave incredible service to other beings to alleviate their suffering, and how parents who really care about their children will nurture them and do everything for their well-being—that is real kindness. Genuine kindness has no ulterior motive.

> *Kind words can be short and easy to speak,*
> *but their echoes are truly endless.*
> **—Mother Teresa**

It's amazing to have a mother who cares for you and nurtures you. My mother is definitely a symbol of love. In Tibet, we generally say that a mother with only one child is the ultimate symbol of how much an individual can care and give love and nurture.

In parenting—as much as in the situation with the thieving beggar—the way we set boundaries is very important. We must use our wisdom to be calm and firm at the same time. We must mean what we say when we set our boundaries, and the other person must know we mean it. At the same time, we should not lose our calm or compassion. If we lose these when dealing with our children, if we start yelling and become aggressive, then our children could feel unloved and become our enemy one day. If, on the other hand, we show firmness while showing kindness, not anger, then the boundary we're setting and the lesson we're teaching to our children can be taken seriously. As well, in situations with people who are possibly trying to take advantage of us, we can set our boundaries with firmness and compassion.

We must consider karma as well. When we are setting boundaries with others, we must consider not just our own karma but others', too. Certain elements are very hard to change because of a person's karma. Another point from the Buddhist perspective is what we call afflictive emotion or defilements of the mind. This is the root of all suffering; all negative karma comes from ignorance, anger, greed, and jealousy. All those dark aspects of the human mind create all the suffering. As long as these inner defilements are in the human mind, we are bound to have problems. In order to transform that, we must transform the human consciousness and become more enlightened, go beyond anger, hatred, greed, jealousy, and all these inner defilements. Then there won't be any problems, but that is a very tall order to achieve.

The Concept of Karma

While some confuse the concept of karma with destiny, karma deals with the concept of cause and effect. Humans act of their own free will, so karma is not fate. It is the sum of all our actions and related reactions from all our lives (if you believe in previous lives). All this determines our future and what we deserve in this life.

According to the Indian yogi and author Paramhans Swami Maheshwarananda, our karma comes from four sources:

- Thoughts
- Words
- Our own actions
- Actions we request others to do

Everything we have ever thought, spoken, done, or caused factors into our karma. When we consider this, everything we do—whether in our mind or in the world—affects our level of joy. The theory of karma goes much deeper—into the actions that separate higher states and lower states—but in this discussion of kindness, it is important to acknowledge the foundational meaning of karma and the meaning of our actions.

Afflictive Emotions

Afflictive emotions is the term used to refer to any negative emotion, including greed, jealousy, desire, hatred, and pride. Negative emotions are actually associated with the right side of our brain, which also controls the secretion of stress hormones. Studies have shown that negative emotions cause the secretion of these hormones, if this side of the brain is continuously active. While these risks are the same for both sexes, higher levels of testosterone seem to exacerbate these hormone secretions, causing a tendency to feel the need to control situations, which often leads to verbal and even physical confrontation.

Afflictive emotions often inspire thoughts like "How could that person do that?" The truth is, however, that we rarely stop to wonder how our response to something is affecting our wellbeing as well as that of those around us. When we can recognize our afflictive emotions before we act on them, we are combating more than just overreactions that we will want to apologize for later. His Holiness the Dalai Lama has said, "Afflictive emotions—our jealousy, anger, hatred, fear—can be put to an end. When you realize that these emotions are only temporary, that they always pass on like clouds in the sky, you also realize they can ultimately be abandoned."

Even Buddha is not able to transform *all* these emotions in the world. Christ was not able to do it. Krishna was not able to do it. You name the entity, he or she hasn't been able to do it. They have all come and gone, and human beings are still here with these afflictive emotions.

We can, however, acknowledge, "I've done everything I can," and then find acceptance and peace of mind. That's what the Dalai Lama really personifies. He's doing everything he can for the Tibetan situation and for religious harmony in the world. Wherever he goes, he speaks about acceptance and peace of mind and conducts interfaith services. He always works to inspire humanity about the value and importance of kindness and tolerance in the world. He's trying his best to make this world more harmonious and peaceful. Because of his great compassion, he chooses to deal with all kinds of problems and suffering every day. At the same time, he is very cheerful and uplifting because of his wisdom and the way he sees reality: that kindness and peace of mind are achievable.

Kindness Profile: Archbishop Desmond Tutu

During the 1980s, Desmond Tutu (1931–) became a name known worldwide for his activism concerning South African apartheid—a system of legal racial segregation that was enforced in South Africa until 1994, causing the black majority to be curtailed and governed by the white minority. Born in 1931, in Klerksdorp, South Africa, Tutu began his professional life as a teacher and eventually went into the study of theology. He was the first black bishop of Johannesburg, and he also became the first black archbishop of Cape Town. In building his career with kindness and compassion, Tutu's responsibility expanded beyond himself to all those suffering in South Africa.

Tutu is often referred to as the voice of the voiceless black people who suffered racial discrimination in South Africa. Through his lectures and writing, he has actively campaigned against apartheid and fought to end AIDS, poverty, and racism. Desmond Tutu was the head of the Truth and Reconciliation Commission and is currently chairperson of The Elders—an independent group of leaders who "offer their collective influence and experience to support peace building, help address major causes of human suffering, and promote the shared interests of humanity." The group was brought together by Nelson Mandela and includes Jimmy Carter, Aung San Suu Kyi, and Kofi Annan.

◌   ◌   ◌

Just as Archbishop Tutu's responsibility became bigger than he was, when we become loving and compassionate, our responsibility in life becomes bigger—it encompasses all humanity, all beings. That means that the greater our responsibility becomes, the wiser we need to become.

We can also adjust our perspective by imagining ourselves in someone else's situation. I once went for a train ride, and the ticket master was very rude. I thought, "Why is he so rude?" I was a bit disturbed, but I didn't say anything. I caught myself becoming upset, and I immediately tried to be in his shoes. I realized that maybe he'd had a really bad time that morning. Maybe something had happened that made him really unhappy—maybe his rudeness wasn't about me. He was really miserable because something else had gone wrong. As soon as I thought of it in that way, my uncomfortable feelings just went away. How we look at situations can make a big difference in life.

> *The first question which the priest and the Levite asked was:*
> *"If I stop to help this man, what will happen to me?"*
> *But . . . the good Samaritan reversed the question:*
> *"If I do not stop to help this man,*
> *what will happen to him?"*
> —**Martin Luther King Jr.**

Meditation Tool: Embracing Kindness

This practice is inspired by Navajo tradition taught by Rudy, a Navajo and Ute peace leader who also works for the PeaceJam

Foundation. The tradition is very beautiful, and I have added to it with my phrase, "May all be kind to each other."

Do this exercise with other people. Standing in a circle, look into each other's eyes. If there are only two of you, simply face each other. Then recite "May all be kind to each other" three times, incorporating the following movement with each successive recitation:

- Left handshake
- Hug with your right arm
- Keep embracing while you feel kindness flowing through you

You can then change partners and continue reciting, shaking hands, hugging, and channeling kindness.

As you do each of these actions, you also want to visualize spreading your positive feelings through your hand toward everyone. Send that positive energy out into the world. Then imagine the people in the world—the politicians, the businesspeople, everyone—affected by this energy. It can be a beautiful visualization.

A variation of this exercise that works for large groups is to stand in a circle while everyone holds the hands of the two people next to them. After grasping hands, start chanting

"May all be kind to each other," and slowly soften your voices until you fade into silence. You will be able to feel the energy of kindness in the room, and as it settles, you can feel peace settling over you.

○ ○ ○ ○ ○ ○ ○ ○ ○

PeaceJam Foundation

Ivan Suvanjieff and Dawn Engle, two extraordinary, innovative beings, had an amazing idea to put Nobel Peace Prize winners and young people together. Through the official representative, they were granted an audience with the Dalai Lama in India. He liked their idea and he said he would participate, but he also wanted them to involve other Nobel Peace Laureate friends to give young people the opportunity to study their lives and get many different perspectives on the world. In brief, this is how the PeaceJam Foundation came about.

"The mission of the PeaceJam Foundation is to create young leaders committed to positive change in themselves, their communities and the world through the inspiration of Nobel Peace Laureates who pass on the spirit, skills, and wisdom they embody."

PeaceJam's program is built on a pyramid of three simple ideas: **Education**, **Inspiration**, and **Action**.

Education: The process starts with education, as the students participate in PeaceJam Programs focusing on the lives of the Nobel Peace Laureates. Programs are available for youth ages 5–29 and each program includes components which stimulate critical thinking skills, strengthen research skills, build skills in leadership and nonviolence, and promote personal reflection and growth.

Inspiration: Education is followed up by Inspiration, which comes from meeting the Nobel Laureates at conferences, and connecting with other people working on projects for their communities. Through the firsthand stories provided by the Nobel Laureates, youth will get to know each Nobel Peace Laureate on a very personal level—each story emphasizing the Laureate's choice to stand up for social justice, human rights, nonviolence, and peace.

Action: After being properly inspired, Jammers get out of their seats and into the streets!

—from the PeaceJam Foundation's website, www.peacejam.org

5
Kindness in Motion

Kindness in words creates confidence.
Kindness in thinking creates profoundness.
Kindness in giving creates love.

—Lao-Tse

One of the most powerful ways to nurture our heart—to become more compassionate, kinder, and more loving—is to find inspiration in our life. Everything starts with inspiration. Whether it is music, art, literature, or another source, there are many different ways to be inspired. We can easily see this when we look at creative professions, but such inspiration can happen in any career where people truly feel called to make a change. For example, people who are in politics may have had a strong conviction to fix a problem in their community and were inspired by that conviction, and so they built their career on it. Some people who have inspired me are His Holiness the Dalai Lama, Aung San Suu Kyi, Betty Williams of Ireland, Jody Williams, Óscar Arias, former president of Costa Rica, Rigoberta Menchú Tum, Archbishop Desmond Tutu, and former U.S. president Jimmy Carter.

When I was in school in India, one of my teachers told us the story of Abraham Lincoln, how he was the son of a farmer and lived deep in the woods. Lincoln had to go many miles to attend school, so he often didn't attend at all. He was well-known for borrowing books from neighbors and walking for miles to borrow books because he preferred to learn as opposed to working in the fields. When he was growing up, this was exactly the opposite of how his father was and how he wanted Abraham to be. Still, Abraham stuck with his reading and, at the age of twenty-four, became a political representative and began to study law.

Gradually, because he was so inspired to make change and help others, he became the sixteenth president of the United States. Lincoln faced a presidency with the nation divided—brother fighting brother as the Civil War continued. In the face of this hardship, Lincoln stood up for what he believed, and his inspiration and dedication allowed the nation to benefit from his leadership.

When we become inspired by what we are doing, our happiness and good intentions are reflected in our actions. Just like the Day of Kindness practice, in which we ask ourselves throughout the day if we are doing things kindly, when spreading kindness, we can ask ourselves if we are working and creating with positive intention—whether in our day-to-day job or a creative endeavor we enjoy. Sometimes kindness itself will speak to us, and sometimes we are inspired by spreading kindness and love in a particular way, through a certain medium. Music is that medium for me.

I was in primary school the first time I played the flute. When I was in school, we had a marching band, so I started playing the flute and learning marching songs, and I became inspired, even from that little exposure. I never had a flute instructor, but somehow the flute stayed with me, and I wanted to continue playing. Mostly, I felt very comfortable playing whatever came into my heart and what I was feeling. I didn't like playing others' music; that didn't touch me as deeply, but I felt very comfortable playing whatever I was feeling. I started playing the flute for others, and people started to really take interest in my music. That joy and inspiration I got from this musical part of my life have never stopped.

When I started playing music again as an adult, I realized that I had actually found a stage for the message I wanted to spread, a way to talk to people. People were listening to me, respecting me, and wanted to hear what I had to say. I began to see how I could pass on the importance of kindness to others through my music. The nature of my flute music has always been quite peaceful, and that has made it the perfect vehicle to communicate one of my most important beliefs: universal love and compassion. As I played more and more, I realized that this was what I wanted to share with humanity, and it was how I wanted to share it with humanity; people can listen and become happier, more peaceful, and kinder. Music as an art form does something to our hearts; it draws certain attention. And with that, we can include a deeper message of love and compassion.

Kind words are the music of the world.
—Frederick Faber

Music is only one type of vehicle we can use to inspire goodwill in others. If you are a filmmaker, you could make a film with kindness as your intention, and you would be creating something that inspires kindness in others. I've seen many movies that inspire me, and that inspiration is available for you, too, if you can look in surprising places. Even comedies can send a positive message. For instance, *Groundhog Day* is one of my favorite films. It's a comedy, but within it is a beautiful message. In the beginning, Bill Murray's character is inconsiderate and cold; he is having a miserable time, making all his colleagues miserable as well. He is self-centered, but then slowly, he starts to become kinder and more generous to everybody around him, and people start to actually enjoy his presence. In this way, that movie accurately illustrates how going through life happy and warmhearted brings happiness to everyone around you. We need more films like this.

Some films that inspire me are *Groundhog Day*, *Pay It Forward*, *Life Is Beautiful*, and *Gandhi*. Any movie about great people such as Martin Luther King Jr., Mother Teresa, His Holiness the Dalai Lama, Desmond Tutu, or other Nobel Peace Laureates and inspiring great leaders are good to watch.

Hopefully, you will find some inspiration from this book, the above films, or music that will be useful and that you will be eager to share with your family and friends. If you're a teacher, you can talk about compassion in your class. I met a schoolteacher who told me that she shares tools to nurture kindness in her students. She calls the lesson the Virtue of Compassion, and you can teach this kind of lesson, too. Reading this book, you have learned many ways that compassion is a virtue, so hopefully these tools will inspire you to inspire others.

If everyone who had the ability to inspire others did so, this would be a kind and tolerant world. Think about all the film-score composers, directors, and playwrights and the power they hold over their audiences. It is easy to see how it would truly be great if more was created with kindness in mind. You can write a poem or a song; you can think of composing a score that will inspire love, kindness, and compassion. If the power that each of us has is used in the right way, we can inspire everyone around us with everything we do.

Humans have incredible brains; among all species on this planet, we have this brain that allows us to understand so many things and be able to create. Even if you think about the houses we live in, we can see that no other species has been able to come up with the complex idea to make the house cooler on hot days and warmer on cool days. This and other luxuries have been created by our thoughts, our ideas, our technologies. Other species can't do that, right?

Our brain lets us think about events that are one hundred years in the future. We are able to plan what is to come, or we can study what happened thousands of years ago. What's amazing is when you think that thousands of years ago, we humans thought to leave all these records and learn an incredible system of language. We have all these languages and different kinds of literature. Truly take a moment to ponder the human brain and all the different creations of art, spirituality, and culture it has created. We can use this intelligence to be a force of happiness and to consciously bring out love, compassion, and kindness.

It is not enough to have a good mind.
The main thing is to use it well.

—René Descartes

One interesting story of creation is that of the Tibetan language and literature. We have a very unique way of writing our alphabet, but its origin is Sanskrit from India. We learned the language and the literature from India, and we brought it with us to Tibet. Tibetan King Songtsen Gampo sent his minister Thumi Sambhota to India to learn the Sanskrit language and then to create Tibet's own alphabet. There were six letters that he couldn't figure out, though, so he went to bed, and he had a dream. In the dream, he met a person who spoke this different language, and he received the six missing letters. So we have thirty consonants.

Tibetan literature is regarded as one of the top ten volumes of literature in the world. Approximately one hundred volumes of Buddha's teachings have been translated into Tibetan. There are also three hundred volumes by the great Indian *Siddhas*, or masters, that interpret Buddha's teachings. These all are translated from Sanskrit into Tibetan. So you can look at this one type of creation and see how unique and highly evolved it is, and that's just one story of many.

This is an amazing story, both of divine inspiration and of creation. Anything we pursue opens our heart and inspires us to do more. If someone wants to become a rabbi or a priest or a monk, things have happened in his or her life that inspire him or her to become that. I was inspired to become a monk in my younger years; now I can find inspiration in movies, music, and writing. My main inspiration, besides kindness, is music, which is perhaps because I have had the honor of being exposed to all different kinds of musicians throughout my life.

I find inspiration in reggae, jazz, blues, rock 'n' roll, country, bluegrass, Bollywood music, folk, rap, Chinese, Japanese, and other Asian, African, European, and Middle Eastern music. Of course, I am also inspired by Tibetan music and songs, especially spiritual songs. Tibet is rich with these, and I would love to explore more in this field in my life.

The Italian classical flutist Andrea Griminelli, who was the primary flutist for operatic tenor Luciano Pavarotti, is amazing. He studied under French composer and flutist Jean-Pierre Rampal and Irish flutist James Galway. Griminelli and I connected through a mutual friend and ended up meeting in Italy, and we started to play together. It was the first time we'd collaborated, and we had no idea what we were going to play—just what key the flute was in—but it was incredible. We played for more than forty minutes straight, and what came out really inspired me. It truly meant something to me to play with a musician of that stature. Griminelli has trained over the years with classical musicians, while my background is the opposite: I have had no training. But we were able to play together, and that was amazing to me. It showed me that one doesn't need to have even the same kind of training—or any training, really—to become inspired and to create something beautiful with others.

The Native American premier flutist R. Carlos Nakai and composer and pianist Peter Kater have also inspired me, and I've had the joy of playing with them. Also, the Japanese musician and composer Kitaro and I did some recording and touring together, which was amazing. Philip Glass and I have played together many times, even at Carnegie Hall several times. He's one of the main Western avant-garde composers and pianists that I love. But I also like and can find inspiration for creating music when I listen to the Beastie Boys, the Beatles, John Lennon, Joan Baez, Bob Marley, and Stevie Wonder. I really love Michael Jackson as well. He was an incredible artist. Some songs like "Thriller," for instance, may have really influenced my composition.

Basically, you can look anywhere for inspiration. I encourage you to look at things that you already love, such as art, dance, or books, and find pieces that not only inspire your own creativity but also evoke a feeling of kindness or convey a story of generosity.

One Indian musician, Ustad Sultan Khan, was a master of the Indian instrument called the *sarangi*, and we played together a few times. That was an amazing experience for me. There I was, inspired by and playing with someone who played an instrument many people have never even heard of. This can happen so easily. Many Westerners are inspired by classical music, but although music has been a lifelong passion for me and I am largely recognized as a musician, I did not grow up with this kind of music. It was not until I was an adult that Tsering Wangyal, former editor for the *Tibetan Review*—the main English newspaper for Tibetans in exile—introduced me to classical music. I met him in New York, and he recommended Mozart's Flute Concertos to me, and I was amazed. There I was, a flute player who had never heard those incredible pieces before that day.

If we look, we can find inspiration in many different places, both expected and unexpected. This occurs in science and art. The story of Isaac Newton's inspiration for his theory of gravity is widely known and even sometimes used in funny situations, but he was actually inspired by watching a simple, natural movement—an apple falling to the ground.

Kindness Profile: Isaac Newton

Though often portrayed as actually being hit on his head by a falling apple, Sir Isaac Newton (1643–1727) often told the story of watching an apple fall from a tree, which made him theorize that gravity existed. Newton's theory of gravity has been the basis of and inspiration for many scientific discoveries and technologies since, thereby making that one apple the foundation on which all subsequent creations were made. Newton's apple inspired others as well, such as writers Alexander Pope, William Wordsworth, and Voltaire, who wrote about it in *Essay on Epic Poetry*, not to mention William Blake's engraving of Newton and the myriad of recent books and films that use Newton as a character or a plot point. Newton and his apple have truly inspired more than anyone could have predicted.

Library of Kindness

In the spirit of the long reach of inspiration, I encourage you to begin a Library of Kindness. The idea is to have a corner in your home where you keep books, DVDs, CDs, art—basically anything that inspires love, kindness, and compassion in you. Your favorite speeches by inspiring people or beautiful paintings and poems on love and compassion can be included. And when you have some time, watch them, listen to them, read them. There are so many different things that you can include, and just as I've shared a list of some inspiring films and music,

I would like to also suggest a few books to start your Library of Kindness:

- *Ethics for the New Millennium* by His Holiness the Dalai Lama
- *The Art of Happiness: A Handbook for Living* by the Dalai Lama and Howard C. Cutler
- *Book of Love and Compassion* by the Dalai Lama
- *Love: The Words and Inspiration of Mother Teresa*
- *Dream: The Words and Inspiration of Martin Luther King, Jr.*
- *No Future Without Forgiveness* by Desmond Tutu
- *Destructive Emotions: How Can We Overcome Them? A Scientific Dialogue with the Dalai Lama* narrated by Daniel Goleman
- *Peace Is Every Step: The Path of Mindfulness in Everyday Life* by Thich Nhat Hanh
- *The Kindness Handbook: A Practical Companion* by Sharon Salzberg
- *PeaceJam: How Young People Can Make Peace in Their Schools and Communities* by Darcy Gifford
- *PeaceJam: A Billion Simple Acts of Peace* by Ivan Suvanjieff and Dawn Gifford Engle

These suggestions are just that—suggestions to get you started—but it's important that you open your heart to the many different sources of motivation to look at kindness every day as the only way to live life happily. His Holiness the Dalai Lama treasures a universal compassion poem that continually inspires him:

Jisi Namkha Nyey-pa Dang,
Drowa Jisi Nyey-gyur Paa,
Deysi Dakni Nyey-gyur Ney,
Drowae Dook Nyal Saylwar Shok.

which translates to:

For as long as space endures,
For as long as sentient beings are there,
May I remain until then,
And solve the suffering of these beings.

Art, in all its forms, transcends differences and brings people together because it illustrates aspects of humanity in ways that we don't see on our own. When you see something in a new way, you break through some of the barriers in your heart. While you are in the process of opening your heart and cultivating kindness, going beyond conditions is part of what will help you achieve bodhicitta. Seeing life, beauty, and truth from a different point of view is one way you can put yourself in somebody else's shoes. By giving you the ability to understand what someone else has had to deal with, you begin to cultivate your empathy.

Kindness Profile: Elie Wiesel

Elie Wiesel (1928–) is known by many Americans as the author of *Night*, which is based on his experience during World War II when he was sent to Buchenwald, the Nazi concentration camp near Weimar, Germany. Not only does Wiesel give voice to those who suffered and survived the Holocaust, but he has also dedicated his life to helping all repressed peoples. According to the Norwegian Nobel Committee, his "message is one of peace, atonement, and human dignity."

Adopted by many high schools as required reading, *Night* has inspired countless readers and opened up a small part of the Holocaust survival experience to those who would never understand it otherwise. Rather than focus on the horrors of the experience, Wiesel has pursued a career and personal life that poetically contribute to literature, theology, and peace. In 1986 Wiesel was awarded the Nobel Peace Prize for "emerg[ing] as one of the most important spiritual leaders and guides in an age when violence, repression and racism continue to characterize the world," proving just what inspired and inspiring art can do.

○ ○ ○

When you decided to read this book, you did so with the specific goal of inspiring and awakening kindness in yourself. When you pick up any other book, CD, DVD, or source of information, you should do so with the same thought in mind. It is through active intention—and being constantly inspired— that we continue to open our hearts. As you are inspired by things, add them to your Library of Kindness, and as you add items created by others, consider creating some of your own. Write a poem, a story, or a piece of music that inspires you or illustrates kindness. Draw something that allows your mind to settle on love and compassion. It is like when you cook a meal for someone you care for—the phrase is "made with love." Make things with love whenever and wherever you can so that you are constantly putting kindness into motion.

With all these different tools, you are trying to learn and be inspired. You do not need to make your Library of Kindness like a museum collection. Some people collect different beautiful things—antiques or expensive artwork—and then put them somewhere in their home where they don't want people to touch them and where they think they will be "safe." This is not that kind of thing. The Library of Kindness is something we learn from by really putting it into practice in our lives, so you want to be able to have things that you can take out and look at, hold, and lend to people. This library can start right in your home and be a constant reminder that tolerance and goodwill are not too idealistic; they are something we can put into practice every day.

Kindness Profile: Mother Teresa

Mother Teresa (1910–1997) is widely known as a humanitarian and a missionary to the extent that she has been nominated for sainthood. While her care for the poor and sick is widely recognized, many don't realize that she started the Missionaries of Charity. What began with thirteen members in 1950 has grown to more than four thousand missionaries that help run orphanages, hospices, and charity centers worldwide.

Mother Teresa was awarded the Nobel Peace Prize in 1979—for which she refused the banquet and instead had the money donated to the poor in India. She put others' needs first in a number of ways—negotiating a ceasefire in 1982 between Palestinian and Israeli forces to free thirty-seven children stuck in the front lines, assisting radiation victims at Chernobyl, and traveling to a number of war zones with the Red Cross to help those in need. Mother Teresa's calling was Christianity, but what she referred to as her "call within the call" was helping the poor while living among them. Mother Teresa lived to see the creation of 450 centers around the world that administered to "the poorest of the poor."

While not everyone can devote their lives to kindness and the service of others in this way, it is all the more important to share these types of stories so that everyone can see just how much we human beings are capable of loving others. Mother Teresa knew it was important to understand what it felt like to be in others' shoes, and she embraced this by living in poverty to help those in poverty.

These inspiring people—artists, politicians, or enlightened beings—have all inspired my life, and by sharing their stories here, I hope you begin to be inspired, and I hope you have begun to think of things to add to or create for your own Library of Kindness.

When we acknowledge that all of life is sacred and that each act is an act of choice and therefore sacred, then life is a sacred dance lived consciously each moment.

When we live at this level,
we participate in the creation of a better world.
—Scout Cloud Lee

Meditation Tool: Harmonic Movement

Harmonic Movement is a meditative, contemplative motion. It looks a little bit like tai chi, and you may consider doing that from time to time as well, as it is a beautiful and peaceful movement. The inspiration for this meditation is twofold. A long time ago, when I was in southern India, I was staying on a beach, and in the early morning there would be these huge rocks that you could get to when the tide was out. I would go out there and meditate on one of the rocks. I really enjoyed sitting in this spot very early in the morning, and when the tide came in, there was a really beautiful movement of the water.

I didn't know how to describe what I saw, but it was truly beautiful, so I called it harmonic movement, and then I found out that tai chi practitioners do a similar movement. It is also performed in a certain kind of yoga, and modern contemplative dance does something similar, too.

This is a dance of yoga, in a way. We like movement in our lives; it's part of our natural human quality. We do different movements in this meditation, and it is a nice way to utilize our physical movement in meditation and contemplation. Concentrating on a peaceful movement helps us enhance our inner peace and find the nurturing nature within us. You can complement this practice with music (use quiet music to accompany your very gentle physical movement). You can create steps and hand movements in any way you are inspired. This movement is very free-form. You can watch others' movements for inspiration to create your own.

Do different physical movements with your hands, your feet, and your posture. The two most important elements here are:

1. The movement should be very gentle and peaceful. Move slowly, tuning your mind to your peaceful, gentle, creative movement.
2. Your mind needs to connect with your movement. It should observe and be with that movement. When you find that your mind is tuned in to your peaceful motion, you'll find more inner stillness—peace.

There should be a nice balance when you are creating; the creativity in your mind is there in your movement. You don't want to be too reserved and involved in the thinking and creation. Feel it. You want a lot of feeling here.

Meditation Tool:
Universal Dance of Kindness

This practice was inspired by the Sufi Dances of Universal Peace, which are performed in a circle in the company of other dancers. The dancers are assisted by a leader who plays a percussive or stringed instrument as a dance accompaniment—though this is not necessary in the Universal Dance of Kindness. The Dances of Universal Peace incorporate different chants, which are religious phrases. In the Universal Dance of Kindness, I use the phrase "May all be kind to each other."

What is alike about these two dances is that participation is key regardless of ability. I like the eye contact and the circle formation while partners rotate; it's very beautiful. And hopefully, when you look into each other's eyes, you can really feel kindness and love.

1. In a large group, create two circles of people—one inner circle facing those in the outer circle. Peaceful and gentle music is a nice accompaniment.
2. Facing your partner in the other circle, say "May all be kind to each other" while looking into each other's eyes.

3. Repeat the phrase for the second recitation while holding hands and continuing to look into each other's eyes. Hold for the third recitation, feeling the kindness spreading out to your partner through your hands.

4. Rotate the inner circle clockwise and the outer counterclockwise, reciting the phrase a fourth time as you change partners.

5. Repeat steps 2 through 4 until you have completed the dance with everyone in your facing circle.

When you practice this with a few people, you don't have to form two circles, but you will want to hold hands with each person and look into each other's eyes while saying the phrase three times. If you have only two people participating, feel free to move together with mindful, peaceful, harmonic movement as you recite, "May all be kind to each other" and look into each other's eyes.

If you are alone somewhere and wish to practice this Universal Dance of Kindness:

1. If you have the facility to play some peaceful and gentle music, do so.

2. Imagine you are chanting "May all be kind to each other" with all humanity. You can chant aloud or just in your imagination.
3. During the first three recitations, imagine you are sending out kindness toward all humanity and toward all other species who also share this planet with us.
4. Then during the next three recitations, imagine you are receiving kindness energy from all beings. You can repeat this sending and receiving in kindness energy as much as you wish, and the recitation can be accompanied with harmonic movement.

6

Love, Kindness, and Compassion in the World

This we know: the earth does not belong to man; man belongs to the earth. All things are connected like the blood that unites us all. Man did not weave the web of life; he is merely a strand in it. Whatever he does to the web, he does to himself.

—**Chief Seattle**

The food we eat and the air we breathe come from the earth. Because of these things, we are alive. We are part of this planet, and we share it with other human beings and other species. The basic reality of life is that we humans are only one of the species that want to live and survive and thrive on this planet, and we need to try to take care—of ourselves, of each other, and of all sentient beings.

Awakening kindness in our hearts can be easier than we think; the feeling is there, just waiting to be developed. Reading this book and using these tools to reacquaint yourself with the significance of this feeling are important steps in becoming a more tolerant and selfless person. Continuing to foster this feeling can be difficult, however. Creating any new habit is difficult—as many people who attempt to diet, quit smoking, and so on, know—even if it is something that benefits you as much as or more than it benefits others. Equipped with the wisdom and tools here, hopefully it will be easy for you to find inspiration and to see kindness in the world around you. For all of us, it is our responsibility to focus on nurturing this feeling; just as kindness itself won't fall from the sky, learning about nurturing these feelings must come from our own inspiration and conviction. No one else will do it for us.

How many governments really focus on helping people grow compassion, love, and kindness? Although we have a great education system in the United States, it is mostly geared toward material development. Spiritual and religious centers don't normally focus on compassion, either. They tend to focus on the tenets of the religion's belief system and specific dogma. Although kindness and tolerance are often taught, awakening and sustaining those feelings are not the focus day after day. One of the most important lessons in life is to nurture and grow love and compassion in our hearts. When we begin to do this, we connect with each other from our hearts. And if we can do that, something happens; the world starts to look more beautiful because we appreciate each other and all sentient beings more.

The interdependent nature of life is a large element of Buddhism, and it's an important focus for remaining kind to everything. What Native Americans say is true: we are not above the Earth; we are a small part of it. Being kind to the Earth and other sentient beings is just as important—and just as beneficial to ourselves—as being kind to other humans. Enlightened beings don't harm other sentient life, and we should all aspire to this. In everything we do, we should try our best to do it kindly.

In the previous chapter, we looked at creative and powerful professions more specifically, but imagine all people are kind in the different work they do in life. One of my favorite stories is from when I lived in the Flatbush area of Brooklyn. There was one postal clerk who displayed exceptional warmth and kindness. He was kind to anyone who went to his window, and when I was in line, I always chose to go to him. And it occurred to me that he had to do this eight-hour job anyway, but because he was kind and serving and warmhearted, I really felt like he was having the time of his life while he was working at this window. He affected whoever went to that window in some little way. Even an unhappy person must have been affected by his kindness a little bit; I know I was each time I went there. This is just a small example of how people in any profession can make a difference when they act from kindness.

If everyone were sympathetic and good-hearted, the world would be very different than it is now. We could enjoy all the details of any situation we experience, fully aware of the kindness of the many who were involved in creating those details. At work, if people were kinder to each other, we would experience more happiness immediately. Looking around at nature, we could appreciate every aspect of our surroundings and the years involved in the creation of each detail. In crowds, we could see the kindness in the little ways people deal with each other. Kindness can improve our quality of life, no matter where we are.

> *Be kind, for everyone you meet*
> *is fighting a hard battle.*
> **—Plato**

I have given workshops and classes in prisons over the years. The Limon Correctional Facility, a maximum-security prison in Colorado, is one of the prisons where I have gone to play music and talk about kindness with the prisoners and guards. I even offered to do one-on-one sessions if anyone from the audience wanted to talk to me. One man who the guards said was the strongest prisoner there wanted to have a one-on-one with me. He was in Limon because he'd killed somebody, and he had killed two more people in prison. So there was this incredibly dangerous man who'd killed three people, and he wanted to have a one-on-one with me to discuss kindness. It was amazing that he saw the value of this and wanted to talk about it more.

During the meeting, he told me he had accepted that he would be in prison for the rest of his life, but he wanted to know if he could do anything in prison to better his life. I said that if he could give protection to the weaker prisoners, it would be a good thing. I have seen documentaries and read articles about prison suffering, and prisoners have a constant fear of violence and bullying. Studies have shown that even prisoners who committed smaller infractions or nonviolent crimes often come out hardened because of bullying. They have to become mean and tough to deal with the violence, and they actually end up psychologically scarred and more violent than they were when they went in. I felt that since this man had the gift of physical strength, he could provide protection to the weaker prisoners. He agreed that in doing that, he would be improving his own life as well as the lives of others. He told me that he would begin practicing this new path in life.

o o o o o o o o o

Looking at Prisons from Another Angle

The government spends, on average, $35,000 annually to house a single prisoner. This is the average across the country, though specific numbers are even more telling. For instance, the state of Maine spends $17,000 more on each inmate than it does on the salary of one public school teacher. Over the years, rehabilitation programs in prisons have fallen in priority due to how many prisoners the United States houses in any given year. More than two million people are incarcerated at any time in the United States, meaning that around $60 billion is spent every year on keeping people in prison, with less and less money spent on rehabilitation and reintegration into society. When we look at the amount of money spent in this regard, it is even more depressing that there is so little focus not just on rehabilitation but on any sort of good we can do in society.

○ ○ ○ ○ ○ ○ ○ ○ ○

Though I suggested that this prisoner defend others, I did not specifically suggest that he stop people by being aggressive and violent. When it can be done, problems should be addressed in a nonviolent manner. I emphasize "when it can be done" because sometimes problems have to be handled with more force. There are times you have to say, "Enough is enough." Sometimes other things won't work.

I met a German man in India a long, long time ago. He had a very good heart, but he saw all the wrong things going on in this world, and he was very unhappy and depressed. He hardly ever smiled. He always seemed frustrated, so I spent a lot of time with him. We spent many hours together talking. After some time, he changed. He started smiling more, and he calmed down. My kindness helped him change, little by little.

At that time, I shared a more serious Buddhist perspective. I explained to him that for as long as our mind is influenced by anger, greed, and ignorance, we are bound to cause suffering toward oneself and others. And how we believe in karma, karmic consequences, and cause and effect. Whatever we experience is based on our own deeds, and that applies to everyone's deeds, be they compassionate, inconsiderate, or apathetic. In thinking of karma, the best idea in any situation is always to figure out a way to solve the problem peacefully, through nonviolence, just as Martin Luther King Jr. did in this country, Gandhi in India, and the Dalai Lama with Tibet now.

Pioneers in Nonviolent Struggle

Mahatma Gandhi

While Mahatma Gandhi (1869–1948) is recognized around the world as a pioneer of nonviolence and civil disobedience for his work in India's struggle for independence, people do not necessarily know the details about his methods of demonstration. One of the first events that illustrated the power that nonviolent means carries is known as the Salt Satyagraha. *Satyagraha* is a combination of the Sanskrit words *Satya* (truth) and *Agraha* (holding firmly to). The Salt Satyagraha was a march that began on March 12, 1929, with Gandhi and seventy-eight followers and ended April 6, 1929, in mass civil disobedience.

Gandhi and his followers marched more than 240 miles to protest the British Raj salt laws, culminating when Gandhi illegally made salt on the seashore. After the march, millions joined Gandhi in breaking the salt laws by buying or making their own salt as well as boycotting other British goods. Though the Salt Satyagraha didn't seem to have an immediate impact on India's independence, it brought unity to the Indian struggle for independence and legitimacy to Gandhi's claims for independence.

Martin Luther King Jr.

Numerous civil-rights successes were achieved by nonviolent means organized and implemented by Dr. Martin Luther King Jr. (1929–1968). Inspired by Gandhi's nonviolent activism, King traveled to India in 1959. His trip included a visit with the Gandhi family. On March 9, his last night there, after a monthlong visit, he said in a radio address:

Since being in India, I am more convinced than ever before that the method of nonviolent resistance is the most potent weapon available to oppressed people in their struggle for justice and human dignity. In a real sense, Mahatma Gandhi embodied in his life certain universal principles that are inherent in the moral structure of the universe, and these principles are as inescapable as the law of gravitation.

In the Birmingham campaign, King and fellow protestors addressed laws they considered unfair by breaking them in nonviolent ways—what was called nonviolent direct action—causing the Birmingham Police Department to fill the jail with protestors to the point of overflow. After running low on adult volunteers not in jail, King organized what would be dubbed the Children's Crusade, which involved children participating in marches and sit-ins. The Birmingham Police Department responded with violent tactics, spraying the young protestors with high-pressure water hoses and using police dogs. Although King was initially criticized for allowing children to become involved in the protests, in the end, the head of the police department was fired, the laws in Birmingham were changed, and King was highly respected for his perseverance and his confidence in nonviolent means.

His Holiness Tenzin Gyatso, the Fourteenth Dalai Lama

The efforts of His Holiness Tenzin Gyatso have significantly contributed to the Tibetan nonviolent struggle and toward peace around the world. I categorize the Dalai Lama's work toward the nonviolent struggle as the Tibetan nonviolent freedom struggle for religious harmony in the world and the promotion of human values.

Born as a Tibetan supreme leader, the Dalai Lama believes that the six million Tibetans put their hope and trust in him for their freedom struggle. Although their freedom is still a long way from being actualized, in his lifetime he has managed to lead the struggle from a nearly lost cause to a hopeful and admired cause in the world today. Tibetan freedom has become one of the most beloved causes around the world, even among peace-loving Chinese brothers and sisters. China may be a strong force of military might and an economic giant, but the Dalai Lama and Tibet have won the heart of humanity for peace and spirituality.

Having been born as a religious leader, the Dalai Lama has adopted an unwavering commitment to religious harmony through interfaith services, pilgrimages at various sacred places, and conversations with other spiritual leaders to develop a deeper understanding of and respect for their religious beliefs. The Dalai Lama once said that as a Buddhist monk, the first thing he thinks is, How can I contribute to the well-being of humanity? Not, How many people can I convert to Buddhism? What a beautiful, profound, and essential principle for all leaders of different religious faiths.

As a world citizen, the Dalai Lama accomplishes some of his most important work promoting the value of love and compassion through public talks around the world. He is the clear personification of living with the values of universal love and compassion wherever he travels.

If we can transform human hearts through the practice of love and compassion, as the Dalai Lama has been doing for many decades, we are working at the root of all conflict and violence. Such a profound, nonviolent method is a tall order to achieve, but it is the ultimate and universal solution for our human conflicts.

☼ ☼ ☼

Nonviolent, peaceful actions are the best tactic to approach a struggle. Just as my German friend gradually transformed from depressed to happy, by using nonviolent means, we can gradually change many of the injustices in the world. Unfortunately, though, circumstances do sometimes get to the point that we need a stronger measure, such as with Hitler in World War II.

In the Buddhist tradition, we believe that everyone can be transformed sooner or later, but sometimes, in certain circumstances, perhaps the transformation will not be quick enough to save lives that are at risk. So perhaps in the situation with World War II, Hitler needed to be subdued by the power of the Allied Forces that finally affected his troops physically. Sometimes in life, a countermeasure stronger than nonviolence is needed, but the most important thing is to not lose our patience and compassion and to maintain our strength and the courage to act.

All that is necessary for evil to triumph
is for good men to do nothing.
—Edmund Burke

When I talk about using a strong countermeasure, as in World War II, the importance is still to keep compassion and love. Our intent still needs to come from a pure place for the action to be truly good, whether others perceive it that way or not.

Tibetan Legend: Weighing Nonviolence

A Tibetan legend illustrates the struggle in choosing between nonviolence and stronger actions in order to save lives. In ancient times, five hundred merchants went into the ocean to find jewels. They searched and searched and ended up finding many jewels on the way home. One merchant became greedy and jealous and began to think of killing everyone there so he could have all the wealth for himself. Fortunately, there was a merchant there who was a bodhisattva. It was said that the bodhisattva merchant was clairvoyant. There are different kinds of clairvoyance, and the highest level is the ability to see what people are thinking.

The bodhisattva was able to see the greedy merchant's thoughts, and he could also see that there was no other way out. Like Hitler, this person's mind was made up to kill the other merchants. In a situation like this, perhaps the only thing to do is to physically act. The bodhisattva saw only one way to save the rest of the merchants' lives: to take the man's life. But the bodhisattva thought, "If I commit such a sin, I am going to the hell realm." (In Buddhism, we also believe that certain unpleasant environments are based on our harmful actions. There is also a realm filled with happiness, and this is based on our altruistic actions.) So he thought, "I might, because of the karma of this situation, go to the hell realm and suffer for a long time." But the bodhisattva decided that he would go through that suffering in order to stop the merchant's misdeed. He realized that because he had the foreknowledge of the merchant's actions, if he didn't stop the merchant, he would ultimately be as responsible for taking the other 498 men's lives and the suffering it would cause their families as well. With all this consideration, he decided to take the life of the merchant.

The bodhisattva was totally selfless in this. Taking some-body's life is obviously a very strong measure, but he did it with selflessness and completely out of compassion for the 498 men the merchant was going to kill. It's very clear: in that circumstance, instead of creating negative karma, the bodhisattva actually purified thousands of lifetimes of negative karma with that act because of his pure intentions. Although the act itself was violence, his heart was totally selfless; he was ready to suffer to save the suffering of others. In such a circumstance, we say that a stronger measure, such as that, is permitted.

◎ ◎ ◎

We may think we are free to act however we want, but unless we are kind to each other, we might as well be suffering. The more we have love and compassion in our heart, the more our life seems as though we are walking in a beautiful flower garden whenever we are around people. This includes not turning away when people are suffering. We can see what kindness does for people who are suffering, how concern for their anguish and what they are going through makes a pure light shine through them. Just as we learn more from those who challenge our patience the most, when we feel it is hardest to look suffering in the face is when we understand true compassion.

Kindness Profile: Florence Nightingale

Florence Nightingale's name is synonymous with nursing, but the things that she sacrificed and went up against to pursue her calling are not as well known. At the age of twenty-five, Nightingale (1820–1910) announced her decision to enter nursing due to what she felt was a divine calling. Her family initially didn't approve of her decision, as she was born into a wealthy, upper-class British family, and a profession such as nursing was considered beneath her station (it's reported that, at the time, most nurses were completely untrained women who were often stereotyped as drunks). In spite of this, she stuck to her decision, even rejecting a marriage proposal from a baron because she was concerned that marriage would adversely affect her ability to continue her career as a nurse.

In 1854 the Crimean War broke out, and reports got back to England of the immense suffering and high death rates in British camps. Nightingale left for Crimea later in the year to tend to the sick and wounded at a barrack hospital in Scutari, where she was negatively received by staff already in place. She forged on with the thirty-eight nurses who had accompanied her and instituted new sanitation standards, lowering the death rate. It is here that she became known as the Lady with the Lamp because she would make solitary rounds after the hospital staff had retired each night. During these late hours, she was often seen walking between the beds of soldiers with only her lamp to light the way.

While tirelessly working to improve conditions for sick and injured soldiers, Nightingale constantly put herself in harm's way, contracting Crimean fever, which she never fully recovered from and which earned her the reputation as an Angel of the Crimea. She was the recipient of many awards and much fanfare, but Nightingale continually shied away from them. Instead of keeping any money that was bestowed as part of her awards, she established the Nightingale Training School for Nurses. To this day, nurses take the Nightingale pledge; her strength and goodwill in the face of constant illness, injury, and death continue to inspire generations of nurses and good-hearted humans.

It's amazing how just one nurse could inspire all of Great Britain. Florence Nightingale became an inspiration for the country and went on to inspire people around the world. How did a simple nurse become so extraordinary? The main factor is the purity of her heart. Her compassion inspired her to take care of wounded soldiers while sacrificing the comforts of the life she was born into. These qualities—kindness, compassion, love—transformed this regular person into a great human being. We all can become great beings when we serve others.

As a Buddhist monk, the first thing the Dalai Lama thinks is, How I can be of service to others? It is not, How many people can I convert to Buddhism? If every world spiritual leader were like this, it would be beautiful; we would no longer have religious wars. If people are interested in our religion, we can teach them, but let's not be intolerant of others' religions. It doesn't benefit us or others to feel that our way is the only way and other methods are wrong. We don't have to make everybody believe what we believe. This power struggle is the reason religious wars start. There can be balance. If all the world's spiritual leaders' first thoughts were, How can I serve humanity through my religion or through myself, simply as a human being? then the world would be a different place. In Buddhism, we advise people to learn all wisdom traditions so we can help all sentient beings who are inclined in that specific wisdom tradition.

Serving others may be one person's calling, just as Florence Nightingale was called to nursing, the medical field, and serving the sick and injured. If you feel you are doing something important in your life for the well-being of others, you should keep doing it. Try your best. Many people have come and gone, and there are still so many problems in this world, so much suffering. It's not over. Different circumstances arise naturally, and sometimes it doesn't matter what we do; things still change. We must try our best to solve the problems, resolve the situations, and do everything skillfully. By educating ourselves—

in wisdom traditions, through this book, or in any other field or form that inspires us—we are becoming more aware and communicating these lessons to the world through our actions.

When there is a global disaster—such as the tsunamis, hurricanes, and earthquakes in the recent past, or even something that was done by man—it is easy for us to feel the call to help others. When we see the suffering of so many, all at once, it changes the way we act, prioritize, and even feel. Few hearts can be apathetic to the great shift that happens when so many souls are released or are in pain. We feel the inspiration and the joy when people act in this type of situation; people volunteer to help others whom they have never met during a time when they are facing true hardship. In these situations, we often hear the phrase, "I can't imagine what they are going through." This is not true.

If we truly couldn't imagine what those people were going through, then we wouldn't be there, extending our hand and heart to help. Help manifests from a feeling of deep compassion and beautiful intention when disaster hits. While there is nothing worse than seeing so many people in such great sorrow at the same time, there is nothing more inspiring than seeing the pure benevolence that swells in this type of sorrow's wake. When people band together in disasters, there is no stopping the rapid evolution of their feelings for fellow humans, and there is nothing more beautiful in life than witnessing this. What I hope you have taken from this experience is that people do not have to face great sorrow for us to feel great love for them. We simply have to remember that great feeling for others every single day.

Kindness Profile: Mohawk Angel Boy

A few years ago, I did a workshop for youth with the PeaceJam Foundation. I had been there a few years in a row at this point, and there was this one young boy, sixteen or seventeen years old. He had a crazy-looking Mohawk that was green, red, and blue, and he wore a leather jacket covered with different buttons; he looked like a punk rocker. He was in the PeaceJam program two years in a row, and we spoke for quite some time the second year. He told me that since attending my workshop the year before, he and his girlfriend started every school day holding hands and saying, "May all be kind to each other," and looking into each other's eyes. I was touched and inspired by the fact that he had done this every day for an entire year.

Here was this teenager who looked, externally, like he could have been the wildest kid in the program—but remember, we shouldn't judge people externally—and he had been so inspired by the workshop the year before that he had worked on his heart every day. Even if that was the only point in the day when he actively considered the state of his heart, he dedicated those few minutes to nurturing his heart every morning.

◎　◎　◎

We all have the potential to grow beauty and love in our hearts. When faced with great suffering, we are inspired to band together with others to express this love. If we can do this and show our humanity every day, we can change the world. Awakening kindness and cultivating it can be work, but it's work that you can begin to do right now to bring more joy into your life and to draw more kindness and love to you.

Tibetan Legend: Transformation

We have a classic story in Tibet about a hermit meditator who was actually a very disturbed being at first. In the daytime, he would mug people, and at night, he became a thief and broke into people's homes to steal from them. People were very afraid of him. One day, an old lady asked him for directions.

He was actually very nice to her, and he gave her the directions, but then she asked him who he was. Without thinking, he said his name, and as soon as she realized that she was talking to this greatly feared person, she was so shocked that she had a heart attack and died. After that experience, he realized what a monster he had become. That someone could die simply from hearing his name affected him so deeply that he changed his life completely, gave up everything destructive, and became a monk.

He was then invited to do special prayers with a family, and the host went into the kitchen to get food and drink to offer him. While alone in the room, the monk saw a bag full of jewelry on the table in front of him. Because of his old habit of stealing, even though he had become a monk, he didn't think he could resist, and his hand went inside the bag, almost on its own. As his hand went into the bag, he realized what he was doing, and he screamed, "There's a thief in the room!" The host ran in, where the monk was sitting there with his hand in the bag. The thing is, the monk practiced very hard at being good, but it was still incredibly difficult for him, and he struggled with it all the time.

They say that he had a collection of dark stones and light stones, and at the end of every day, he made a calculation of the good things he had done and all the bad things he had done—

mentally, verbally, or physically—and he would put aside a dark stone for every bad act and a light stone for every good act. In that way, he had a visual reminder of what he was struggling with and how far he was from the kind of person he wanted to be. Gradually, the darker stones became fewer and fewer because he practiced hard and reminded himself to be good every day. The day he realized what kind of person he had become and what kind he really wanted to be, he began trying. I hope now it is the same for you.

❁ ❁ ❁

I can think of no better way to inspire you to start this practice than to leave you with this profound thought:

> *Yesterday is gone. Tomorrow has not yet come.*
> *We have only today. Let us begin.*
> —**Mother Teresa**

Epilogue

My friend, I hope that you have enjoyed the journey of reading my book, that your heart has warmed a little, and that you are inspired by love, kindness, and compassion. You picked up this book because you have a desire to improve your life; and you've read this far, hopefully, because you have realized the true value of these feelings and want to actively awaken and nurture them every day. These inner values are the jewels of humanity. Wherever we go in this world, if we are equipped with these inner jewels, we will always find the other things that make life wonderful: good friends, meaning and purpose, ageless beauty, confidence, a universal spiritual essence, and, above all, joy and peace.

You now have the means to see all humanity as a friend—not as competition—because we are all trying to achieve happiness and avoid suffering. You also inherently feel the value of kindness—toward yourself and others. And with all the tools and meditations I have talked about, you can begin to practice kindness every day. Every morning, you will wake up and want to practice a Day of Kindness because you will begin to see and feel the benefits of these actions. As you cultivate love, kindness, and compassion, your life will evolve in positive ways, and your true nature and beauty will begin to shine through.

Remember that one of the greatest gifts and marvels of being human is that we can choose to consciously nurture and grow love, kindness, and compassion in our hearts. Not only do we have this ability, but we can even expand these precious human values until they become universal and unconditional. Therefore, we must start cherishing these values as one of the greatest parts of our potential and begin to nurture them today, right now. We can start by being kind to ourselves and to those closest to us. There is nothing to lose by trying to tap into this truly wonderful feeling. By doing so, we may just start experiencing some of the wonders, beauties, and meanings I have mentioned during this journey to awakening kindness.

This is the most universal and powerful source of peace and harmony for all humanity and for all other species who also share this planet with us.

I have had teachings from His Holiness the Dalai Lama from my childhood in India and around the world until now, as I age in the West, and the essence of his teachings for humanity always remains the same: the practice of kindness. "If you can help and serve others, try your best. If you can't be that, at least try your best never to hurt or harm others." This is the essence of all great religions and of universal spirituality. It may not always be easy, but we must remember that being kind can become like second nature to us, and the potential to be kind is within us all. We are the ones who must awaken that kindness.

Thank you for letting me be your spiritual friend on this journey. Now it is time for you to begin this practice on your own, but before you do, imagine that we are holding hands and feeling the true value and meaning of kindness. Imagine that this feeling is strengthening and nurturing our hearts as you set off on this amazing adventure—the beautiful practice of kindness—and feel the full power of the phrase, which is blessed and endorsed by ten Nobel Peace Laureates:

May all be kind to each other.

Acknowledgments

From the bottom of my heart, my highest gratitude goes to His Holiness the Dalai Lama, Kyabje Lati Rinpoche, Gen Yeshe Topden, and all my other spiritual teachers from all four Tibetan Buddhist traditions for inspiring and nurturing my heart with wisdom and compassion. Without their teachings on the universal values of kindness, compassion, love, and wisdom, this book could not have been possible.

Another highest gratitude goes to my late mother, Samten Wangmo—my first spiritual teacher—my courageous and warrior father, Yangluk, my kind and gentle elder sister, Sonam Dolma, and a compassionate Acha Kelsong Dolma for bringing me to the land of freedom (India, the great spiritual country) and nurturing me for so many years.

Deep gratitude goes to my book angel, Cynthia Black, editor in chief and cofounder of Beyond Words Publishing, for putting hope and trust in me and publishing my first book. Huge thanks to managing editor Lindsay S. Brown for lending her expertise to make this book better. Special thanks to my editor, Gretchen Stelter, for her helpful guidance and hard work to improve this book. I must also thank Tami Simon, founder and CEO of Sounds True; Judith Curr, publisher of Atria Books; Richard Cohn, cofounder of Beyond Words Publishing; and all the beautiful people at Sounds True, Beyond Words Publishing, and Atria Books for their kindness and hard work.

I also want to express my deep gratitude to my eternal sweetheart, Tsering Youdon, for helping me in the process of writing this book and for giving me the utmost care and love during my recovery from the life-threatening car accident I experienced in India and my heart attack.

My deep gratitude must go to Leslie Christianson—a very kind and beautiful being—for bringing me to a great land of freedom and opportunity (Australia) and for giving such great care and love to our two beautiful children, Sangye and Tenzin. I must also thank my son, Sangye, for saving my life during my car accident, and my daughter, Tenzin, for praying for my life for many days.

I lack the words to express my gratitude to my mysterious blessing and great friend Richard Gere for inviting me to this great land of America and helping me in so many ways. I also want to thank Cory Hodnefield, who helped me with cleaning up lots of messy corrections in my original transcription and who with his wife, Alicia Hodnefield, helped me with some of the earlier editing.

Now I must pay my humble gratitude to these individuals and organizations: Bob and Nina Thurman, Philip Glass, Yangkyi Tsering, Anna Sauza, Ganden Thurman, and Kyra Borre and all the good people at Tibet House, New York; Doboom Tulku Rinpoche and friends at Tibet House, Delhi, India; Sulak Sivaraksa (Nobel Peace Prize nominee and greatest supporter of the Tibetan cause in Thailand) and all the great people who work for Ajan Sulak; Lama Zopa Rinpoche and all the dharma friends at the Foundation for the Preservation of the Mahayana Tradition centers around the world; Hyun Bong Sunim and Sonil Sunim, Lee Mikyung and her son, Jeong Jooyoong, from South Korea for inviting me there and making me successful in their country; Mr. Kang and Mrs. Kim Pil Jo for sponsoring me many times in South Korea; Adam Yauch and the Beastie

Boys and all the incredible people who worked hard at the Milarepa Fund for the historic Tibetan freedom concerts; Smash, a great concert producer in Japan, and the Boss and all the great staff there; Pami Sign, Mina and Chukie Palmo, and all the great people at the International Festival of Sacred Arts in New Delhi, India; Rinchen Phuntsok, Wangpo Bhashe, and the other great Tibetan guy in His Holiness the Dalai Lama's office in Paris; Mrs. Koo (CEO of BTN South Korea), Suk, Sung Woo Sunim (chairman of BTN), Emi Hayakawa (daughter of Mrs. Koo and film narrator), and Mr. Kim Joon-nyeon (film director), all of whom I must thank and for making me more successful in South Korea by making a documentary film on my life story and helping me in many other ways; Dick and Ann Grace (founders of Unsung Heroes Award); Rinchen Dharlo and the Tibet Fund; Tenzin Geche Tethong, one of the most dedicated personal secretaries to His Holiness the Dalai Lama; his most gentle and great Tibetan classical singer Chukie Kelsang Tethong; Kunoe Lobsang Gawa La and Kunoe Peljor La, the two most dedicated personal attendants to His Holiness the Dalai Lama and two beings who were born to serve His Holiness to enhance his work for humanity and all beings; Kunoe Tarak La, the most dedicated personal secretary to serve His Holiness the Dalai

Lama at the right time and who also happens to be a great saint and practitioner of the twentieth century; Kazur Tenzin N. Tethong and Darlene Markovich, the Dalai Lama Foundation, and its wonderful people; Lodi Gyari Rinpoche, Bhuchung Tsering, and all the hardworking friends at the International Campaign for Tibet; and all the past and present friends at the Tibetan government in exile under the great leadership of His Holiness the Dalai Lama during the most tragic and desperate time in our more than two-thousand-year history. I pay my highest respect to you all. You are the fire that has inspired us to keep the struggle burning, and it will continue to burn with our heroes to come. I thank all the Tibetan freedom fighters for your commitment and dedication to our Tibetan freedom struggle. I also must thank from the bottom of my heart the government and people of India for their immeasurable kindness and help given to the Tibetans for the last fifty years.

I owe a huge debt of gratitude to Dawn Gifford Engle and Ivan Suvanjieff and the PeaceJam Foundation's beautiful, hardworking friends, and to Adam Engle and the Mind & Life Institute's wonderful people.

I extend a million apologies to anyone whose name belongs here and was missed; you know who you are, and you have my eternal gratitude as well—you know you do!

Acknowledgments

I am humbled and honored to learn that so many people from around the world prayed for me during my recovery from the car accident in India in 2007. I am still alive and kicking because of you. I want to thank you all from the bottom of my heart, and I hope to spend the rest of my life bringing some useful service to humanity and to all the species who share this planet.

Appendix: Practical Meditation Tools

Posture and Breathing Meditation

Before you begin meditating, think of your meditation posture. You can sit on a chair with back support or on the floor with a cushion or a mat, cross-legged. If you prefer, you can sit in the semi-lotus position, which is on the floor with each leg bent and each foot resting on the opposite leg's thigh. For this beginning meditation, a simple sitting posture is fine.

With all meditations, keep in mind:

- Sit up straight; have a straight spine
- Your back, neck, and shoulders should be relaxed

- Clear your mind so you can be aware and conscious of your meditation

Also be aware of what you are doing with your hands: left on bottom, right on top, both palms facing up and the tips of your thumbs touching. The thumbs should touch somewhere at the level of your navel. There are a few ways to hold your head, but try bending it slightly forward, but not so far that you become sleepy. Allow your eyes to semi-open and gaze out over the tip of your nose. This natural gaze can help you collect all your distracted thoughts into a completely focused state of mind. For a relaxing meditation like this one, you also can close your eyes. Your mouth and jaw should be relaxed and natural as well, so touch the tip of your tongue gently to your upper palate. Your mouth should just be closed naturally.

We all breathe, so this is one of the simplest as well as the most beneficial meditations to begin with. Breathe naturally, through your nose if possible or comfortable. Be aware of the sensation of your breath as it enters and leaves your nostrils. This sensation should be the single-pointed focus of your meditation when you first begin. Try to concentrate on it to the exclusion of everything else.

At first, your mind will be busy, and you might feel your awareness moving. If this happens, you may actually be improving your meditation practice, as you are becoming more aware of how your awareness moves. Try, in spite of feeling your awareness move around, to remain focused single-pointedly on the sensation of the breath. If you find that your awareness has wandered and is focusing on thoughts, surroundings, and so on, immediately but gently return your awareness to your breath. Repeat this whenever you can until your mind settles on your breath regularly.

Set aside some time every day to contemplate your breath or even everyday wonders—the sun shining, the beauty we can find in simple objects—to truly benefit these positive human values in your heart. Then, slowly but steadily, you will truly become inspired by these inner values, and your heart will open. This is when your true humanity starts to take root within your heart and mind. The great master Khunu Lama Rinpoche said, "[Meditation] is how it is possible how an individual can transform his or her heart and become more loving, kinder, and more compassionate."

Day of Kindness

The idea of adopting a day of kindness is like eating a delicious ice cream: once you've tried it, you truly know the delightfulness of the treat. In the same way, if you can experience the wonders, beauty, and meaningfulness of receiving kindness, you may want to be kinder throughout your life. Therefore it could be beautiful to try to practice a Day of Kindness.

From this moment through the next twenty-four hours, adopt a Day of Kindness. The idea for a Day of Kindness is to spend at least one day out of the year really celebrating and focusing on kindness—just as we celebrate different people every year on, for instance, Father's Day or Mother's Day. You can adopt this day at any time, so I suggest making the next twenty-four hours your Day of Kindness. During this day, really try to turn your heart and mind to kindness. Here are some tactics to help you:

- When you're talking to people, ask yourself, "Am I speaking kindly?"
- When you're walking, ask yourself, "Am I walking kindly?"
- When you are doing anything, ask yourself, "Am I doing this kindly?"

This is what bodhisattvas do; they really tune their whole being and all their actions toward not hurting anyone and always trying to benefit others through kindness and servitude.

While you are eating, think about the kindness of all the beings that were involved in making that food: the four elements, the farmers who worked so hard on cultivating it, the people who cooked it, the animals that also lived off the land and/or fertilized it. Think about how much hard work all the beings did and how much care they gave so you could have the food you are eating, and be grateful and say thank you for that. Think about how you've been given a place to sit and this book to read. Many people have worked hard to create the place where you are sitting and this book you are reading, so try to think about that and say thank you. Behind everything, there has been so much hard work, so reflect for an entire day on the kindness of others that has brought you to where you are.

You can also think about or try to engage in these simple kindness practices during the Day of Kindness:

- Try to patch up a strained relationship. Maybe you haven't spoken to a person for years due to some silly mistake or misunderstanding. Send a simple gift with a note or call and say, "I miss you. Please forgive me." You never know what wonders a few kind words can do.
- Share a dollar or two with a homeless person.
- Give a kind smile to a sad and suffering person.

- Become a member of PETA or Amnesty International.
- Write a poem about kindness or think about writing a book or screenplay with a theme focused on love, kindness, compassion, and humor.
- Compose a song about love and compassion.
- If you are a parent or teacher, tell your children or students stories about kindness once a month.
- Make dinner at home for a week instead of going out to eat at a fast-food establishment or restaurant. Donate the money you save to a needy or worthy organization. Eating at home can also be good for your health.

Walking Kindness

The Walking Kindness Meditation is inspired by traditional Theravada and Vietnamese Buddhist walking meditation. You will use the same phrase as in the Breathing Meditation: "May all be kind to each other." Whenever you have time, you can do the Walking Kindness Meditation in your park or in nature or even just when you have the time to go for a quick walk around your block. The famous Buddhist monk Thich Nhat Hanh has made walking meditation very popular.

Walking meditation is a more mindful meditation than one that involves simply breathing, but it is what inspired me to create this new exercise. This tool is very useful because most people walk, so we can fit walking kindness meditation into our everyday lives. Walking from the car into a mall, to a bus stop, through a parking lot—walking just about anywhere can be an opportunity for a walking kindness meditation.

Walking itself can transform the way that we find peace, the way we find kindness and compassion and nurture our hearts. Practicing the walking kindness meditation is part of my workshop. If you can, go somewhere in nature where you don't have to be mindful of traffic and where you can see a beautiful view. When you are walking, just walk very gently. You can also chant "May we all be kind to each other" in the process of walking, either aloud or in your head. You can also walk silently while focusing your mind and listening on your walk, thinking of kindness and compassion.

There are a few key differences between walking kindness meditation and sitting meditation. Obviously, you want to keep your eyes open during walking kindness meditation. This change means there will be other alterations in the way you do the practice. You do not want to draw your consciousness inward in the same way that you do when you practice the Posture and Breathing Meditation outlined earlier. For your safety, you have to be aware of the world outside yourself, obviously, so you don't want to walk with your eyes closed. Also, be aware of your other surroundings—the weather, nature, sounds, and so on—and respond to them accordingly. One very positive difference between walking kindness meditation and sitting meditation is that most people find it easier to be aware of their bodies when they are in motion, so walking kindness meditation can be a very intense experience.

Embracing Kindness

This practice is inspired by Navajo tradition taught by Rudy, a Navajo and Ute peace leader who also works for the PeaceJam Foundation. The tradition is very beautiful, and I have added to it with my phrase, "May all be kind to each other."

Do this exercise with other people. Standing in a circle, look into each other's eyes. If there are only two of you, simply face each other. Then recite "May all be kind to each other" three times, incorporating the following movement with each successive recitation:

- Left handshake
- Hug with your right arm
- Keep embracing while you feel kindness flowing through you

You can then change partners and continue reciting, shaking hands, hugging, and channeling kindness.

As you do each of these actions, you also want to visualize spreading your positive feelings through your hand toward everyone. Send that positive energy out into the world. Then imagine the people in the world—the politicians, the businesspeople, everyone—affected by this energy. It can be a beautiful visualization.

A variation of this exercise that works for large groups is to stand in a circle while everyone holds the hands of the two people next to them. After grasping hands, start chanting "May all be kind to each other" and slowly soften your voices until you fade into silence. You will be able to feel the energy of kindness in the room, and as it settles, you can feel peace settling over you.

Harmonic Movement

Harmonic Movement is a meditative, contemplative motion. It looks a little bit like tai chi, and you may consider doing that from time to time as well, as it is a beautiful and peaceful movement. The inspiration for this meditation is twofold. A long time ago, when I was in southern India, I was staying on a beach, and in the early morning there would be these huge rocks that you could get to when the tide was out. I would go out there and meditate on one of the rocks. I really enjoyed sitting in this spot very early in the morning, and when the tide came in, there was a really beautiful movement of the water.

I didn't know how to describe what I saw, but it was truly beautiful, so I called it harmonic movement, and then I found out that tai chi practitioners do a similar movement. It is also performed in a certain kind of yoga, and modern contemplative dance does something similar, too.

This is a dance of yoga, in a way. We like movement in our lives; it's part of our natural human quality. We do different movements in this meditation, and it is a nice way to utilize our physical movement in meditation and contemplation. Concentrating on a peaceful movement helps us enhance our inner peace and find the nurturing nature within us. You can complement this practice with music (use quiet music to accompany your very gentle physical movement). You can create steps and hand movements in any way you are inspired. This movement is very free-form. You can watch others' movements for inspiration to create your own.

Try out different physical movements with your hands, your feet, and your posture. The two most important elements here are:

1. The movement should be very gentle and peaceful. Move slowly, tuning your mind to your peaceful, gentle, creative movement.
2. Your mind needs to connect with your movement. It should observe and be with that movement. When you find that your mind is tuned in to your peaceful motion, you'll find more inner stillness—peace.

There should be a nice balance when you are creating; the creativity in your mind is there in your movement. You don't want to be too reserved and involved in the creation. Feel it. You want a lot of feeling here.

Universal Dance of Kindness

This practice was inspired by the Sufi Dances of Universal Peace, which are performed in a circle in the company of other dancers. The dancers are assisted by a leader who plays a percussive or stringed instrument as a dance accompaniment—though this is not necessary in the Universal Dance of Kindness. The Dances of Universal Peace incorporate different chants, which are religious phrases. In the Universal Dance of Kindness, I use the phrase "May all be kind to each other."

What is alike about these two dances is that participation is key regardless of ability. I like the eye contact and the circle formation while partners rotate; it's very beautiful. And hopefully, when you look into each other's eyes, you can really feel kindness and love.

1. In a large group, create two circles of people—one inner circle facing those in the outer circle. Peaceful and gentle music is a nice accompaniment.
2. Facing your partner in the other circle, say "May all be kind to each other" while looking into each other's eyes.
3. Repeat the phrase for the second recitation while holding hands and continuing to look into each other's eyes. Hold for the third recitation, feeling the kindness spreading out to your partner through your hands.
4. Rotate the inner circle clockwise and the outer counterclockwise, reciting the phrase a fourth time as you change partners.
5. Repeat steps 2 through 4 until you have completed the dance with everyone in your facing circle.

When you practice this with a few people, you don't have to form two circles, but you will want to hold hands with each person and look into each other's eyes while saying the phrase three times. If you have only two people participating, feel free to move together with mindful, peaceful, harmonic movement as you recite "May all be kind to each other" and look into each other's eyes.

If you are alone somewhere and wish to practice this Universal Dance of Kindness:

1. If you have the facility to play some peaceful and gentle music, do so.
2. Imagine you are chanting "May all be kind to each other" with all humanity. You can chant aloud or just in your imagination.
3. During the first three recitations, imagine you are sending out kindness toward all humanity and toward all other species who also share this planet with us.
4. Then during the next three recitations, imagine you are receiving kindness energy from all beings. You can repeat this sending and receiving in kindness energy as much as you wish, and the recitation can be accompanied with harmonic movement.

Glossary of Terms and Names

afflictive emotions: Negative emotions that cause disharmony within oneself or with others; the emotions we need to overcome

Atisha: A great Buddhist saint who was born an Indian prince and went to Tibet. He died there after seventeen years of living and teaching to the Tibetan people.

Aung San Suu Kyi: Nobel Peace Laureate from Myanmar (formerly Burma). She is still under house arrest for her leadership in the democratic movement in Myanmar.

Bhagavad Gita: Sacred Hindu scripture of seven hundred verses contained within the *Mahabharta*, summarizing Vedic philosophy spoken by Shri Krishna

bodhicitta: An altruistic aspiration to become an enlightened being in order to serve others

bodhisattva: A being who has cultivated bodhicitta

Chamba Valley, Himachal Pradesh, India: Region where Nawang's father worked when Nawang was a boy

Chandragiri, Orissa: Tibetan refugee camp in India where Nawang grew up

Chay-Gom: Analytical meditation

Chenrezig: Buddha of compassion

Choejook Darti: One of the most extensive commentaries on *A Guide to the Bodhisattva Way of Life*—a great teaching on the Mahayana Buddhist path and bodhicitta

Dharamsala: City in India where His Holiness the Dalai Lama lives and has established Tibetan government in exile

Drupchen: Honorific title that means that someone has achieved a vast accomplishment in enlightenment

Ganden: A great monastery in Tibet, established by Lama Tsongkhapa

Gangla Dakgi Fen-takpa, Reywa Cheywa Gang-shik Gi, Shintoo Mirik Noe Jeyna Yang, Shey Nyen Damper Tawar Shok: One of the "Eight Verses for Training the Mind," which translates to "When someone whom I have helped, Or in whom I have placed great hopes, Mistreats me in extremely hurtful ways, May I regard him still as my precious teacher."

Geltey Choe-soo Yoe-nani, Dela Migar Jaychi Yoe, Geltey Choe-soo Mey-nani, Dela Migar Jaychi Feyn: One of the Dalai Lama's favorite sayings, composed by Indian master Shantideva, which translates to "If there is a way or a solution to the problem, what is there to be worried and upset about? If there is no way or solution to the problem, what is the use of being upset about it?"

Geluk: One of the four great Tibetan Buddhist traditions founded by Lama Tsongkhapa

Geshe Langri Thangpa: A great Buddhist master from Khadampa lineage

Geshe Lharampa: The highest qualified Buddhist master (in Geluk tradition)

Golog, Amdo: Region in Tibet where His Holiness the Dalai Lama was born

gom: Familiarization or meditation

Guide to the Bodhisattva Way of Life, A: A great teaching on the Mahayana Buddhist tradition and on cultivating universal love and compassion

Gyomna Laawar, Migyur Wey, Nyoedey Gangyang Yoe Mayin: A phrase from *Guide to the Bodhisattva Way of Life* that translates to "Through familiarity, there is nothing that doesn't get easier."

interdependent nature of life: A main tenet of Buddhism that explains that all beings, things, and events are dependent on other factors and are interconnected

Jampa Chenpo: Great love, love toward all sentient beings

Jisi Namkha Nyey-pa Dang, Drowa Jisi Nyey-gyur Paa, Deysi Dakni Nyey-gyur Ney, Drowae Dook Nyal Saylwar Shok: Universal compassion poem, which translates to "For as long as space endures, For as long as sentient beings are there, May I remain until then, And solve the suffering of these beings."

Jog-Gom: Single-pointed meditation

Kadam Fachoe Buchoe: Buddhist teaching that means "The Doctrine of Father and Son"

Kagyu: One of the four great Tibetan Buddhist traditions founded by Marpa Lotsawa

Kagyu Monastery (Drukpa Kagyu): Monastery where Nawang's mother was a nun

Kham: One of the three regions of Tibet, where Khampas are from

Khampas: One of the warrior tribes of Tibet

Khunu Lama Rinpoche: A great Buddhist master who also became a main Buddhist teacher to the Dalai Lama

Koonsang Lamae Shel-loong: A great Buddhist scripture from Nyingma lineage

Kuno Tarak-la: The Dalai Lama's former principal secretary

Lama Jangsem: A lama and hermit meditator who predicted China's invasion of Tibet to Nawang's family

Lamrim: One of the greatest Buddhist scriptures from the Geluk school tradition

Lamrim Chenmo: Scripture title meaning "The Great Treatise on the Stages of the Path to Enlightenment"

Lhasa: The capital city of Tibet

loong: The energy that moves awareness

Loong Joong Nyoop Ki Gom: Breathing meditation yoga

Milarepa: The most respected and revered Buddhist saint in Tibet from Kagyu lineage

Mussoorie, Uttarakhand: City in India

namshe: Consciousness

Nyingje Chenpo: Great compassion toward all sentient beings

Nyingma: The oldest of the four great Tibetan Buddhist traditions founded by Padma Sambava and Shanta Rakshitak by the request of the great Tibetan King Trisong Dhetsen

Orissa: State in India where Nawang's family lived in exile

Padma Sambava: Indian sage and guru; considered second Buddha by the Nyingma school

Paramhans Swami Maheshwarananda: Indian yogi, guru, and author

Sakya: One of four great Tibetan Buddhist traditions, founded by Sachen Kunga Nyingpo

sam: Contemplating, analyzing

sem: Clarity; awareness

Shakyamuni: The founder of Buddhism; Buddha

Shantideva: An eighth-century great Indian Buddhist master from the famed Nalanda University

Shunyata: Dependent origination or emptiness of inherent existence (the most profound Buddhist wisdom involving the interdependence of everything)

Siddhas: Highly realized Buddhist masters

Songtsen Gampo: One of the greatest kings of Tibet

Theravada tradition: Buddhist tradition from Thailand, Burma, and Sri Lanka

Thich Nhat Hanh: A revered Buddhist master who has taught in the West for many years and has popularized walking meditation

Thoe Sam Gom Soom: The three processes of meditation: learning, contemplating, and meditating

transitory nature of life: A main tenet of Buddhism that states that everything in existence is bound to undergo change

tsolchey: With effort

tsolmay: Effortless

yeshe: Clarity, wisdom

yogi: Advanced hermit meditator

Tibetan Poems

Praising the Values and Wonders of Universal Love and Compassion

(composed by Kuna Lama Rinpoche and translated by Nawang Khechog)

སེམས་ཀྱི་རྩྭ་བ་བྱུང་ཆུབ་སེམས། །སེམས་ཀྱི་ཉི་མ་བྱུང་ཆུབ་སེམས། །
སེམས་ཀྱི་ནོར་བུ་བྱུང་ཆུབ་སེམས། །སེམས་ཀྱི་བདུད་རྩི་བྱུང་ཆུབ་སེམས། །

One which cools the mind and heart like moon is universal
love, compassion, and bodhicitta.
One which brightens the mind and heart like sun is universal
love, compassion, and bodhicitta.
One which enriches the mind and heart like a jewel is universal
love, compassion, and bodhicitta.
One which nurtures the mind and heart like nectar is universal
love, compassion, and bodhicitta.

ཡུལ་དུས་གནས་སྐབས་ཐམས་ཅད་དུ། །རིས་བྲལ་སེམས་ཅན་ཀུན་གྱི་དོན། །
བློ་སྟོབས་རེ་བ་མེད་པར་མཛད། །བྱང་ཆུབ་སེམས་ལ་བརྟེན་ནས་ཡིན། །

The wise one, without any discrimination,
Engages to serve and benefit all sentient beings,
In any circumstances and in all places and times,
With no expectation (whatsoever).
(Such a pure deed is) due to universal love, compassion,
    and bodhicitta.

འཕུར་བའི་ཚོ་ན་ཟིངས་པ་མེད། །རྐྱུད་པའི་ཚོ་ན་ཞུམ་པ་མེད། །
གཞན་གྱིས་རྗེ་བར་མི་ནུས་པ། །རིན་ཆེན་དང་པོའི་བྱུང་རྒྱབ་སེམས། །

You have no arrogance when you are prosperous,
You do not get depressed when things fall apart,
(You become) unharmable by anything—
That is because of your diamond-like (inner quality of)
     universal love, compassion, and bodhicitta.

འཇུངས་པ་གསེར་དང་དངུལ་གྱིས་དགའ། །འདོད་ལྡན་གཟིན་ནུ་མ་ཡིས་དགའ། །
འཕོར་འགྲོ་སྟུང་མའི་རྩི་ཡིས་དགའ། །དམ་པ་བྱང་ཆུབ་སེམས་ཀྱིས་དགའ། །

Misers love gold and silver,
Playboys love young, beautiful women,
Bumblebees love the essence of flowers,
The highly evolved beings love universal compassion, kindness,
    and bodhicitta.

སྲིད་ན་མེད་ཐབས་མེད་པ་ཡི། །ཚོས་ནི་གང་ཞེས་ཏྲོག་པ་ན། །
བྱང་ཆུབ་སེམས་མཆོག་ཁོ་ན་ལས། །གཞན་ཞིག་དམ་པ་སུ་ལ་སྟེད། །

When examined, what could be that
Spiritual value most needed in this universe?
The great beings can find none other than
Universal love, compassion, and bodhicitta.

འགའ་ཞིག་བྱུང་རྒྱབ་སེམས་ཀྱི་དོན། །ཚུལ་དང་མཐུན་པར་འཆད་ཤེས་མོད། །
སྐྱེ་བའི་རྒྱུ་ཚོགས་མ་ཚང་བས། །རང་གི་རྒྱུད་ལ་བྱུང་སེམས་དབེན། །

Some people may be very well versed
In explaining universal love, compassion, and bodhicitta,
But they are actually empty of these spiritual qualities
Because they lack its real cause and condition.

བྱང་ཆུབ་སེམས་ཀྱི་འདབ་བརྒྱ་པ། །ཀུན་ནས་བཞད་ན་མ་བོས་ཀྱང་། །
མ་རྟ་དོན་དུ་གཉེར་བའི་བློས། །འགྲོ་བའི་བྱང་བ་དང་གིས་འདུ། །

When the hundred-petal lotus of universal love, compassion,
    and Bodhicitta blooms (in your heart),
Honeybees, of all living creatures, will be naturally drawn to you—
Even if you don't call out for them—
Simply because they all are seeking the honey
(The real source of happiness and higher spiritual essence).

བྱང་ཆུབ་སེམས་ཀྱི་གནད་ཤེས་ཕྱིར། །ཐེག་པ་ཆེན་པོའི་བཤེས་གཉེན་བསྟེན། །
ཐེག་པ་ཆེན་པོའི་མདོ་སྡེ་བཀླག །བདེ་གཤེགས་སྲས་དང་འགྲོགས་པར་བྱ། །

In order to learn the essential points,
How to cultivate universal love, compassion, and bodhicitta,
One should study from teachers who practice these values,
One should read books which express these inner values,
And (it will inspire you deeply to) befriend those
Who embody these qualities.

Free Music Download

Visit www.beyondword.com/nawangkhechog/ and www.simonandschuster.com/Awakening-Kindness for a free music download showcasing some of Grammy nominee Nawang Khechog's most adored compositions.

Personally handpicked by renowned flutist Nawang Khechog, this compilation will enhance the work you are about to embark upon with *Awakening Kindness*.

Track 1:	1st Movement: Sentient Beings* (*Winds of Devotion*)	5:18
Track 2:	Dance of Innocents* (*The Dance of Innocents*)	7:11
Track 3:	For As Long As Space Endures* (*Tibetan Meditation Music*)	6:39
Track 4:	Healing Through Kindness* (*Music as Medicine*)	5:11
Track 5:	A Sad Return to My Birthplace* (*Quiet Mind*)	4:06
Track 6:	Nobel Peace Laureate* (*Rhythms of Peace*)	6:46
Track 7:	Wanting Peace* (*Sounds of Peace*)	3:28
Track 8:	Five-Peak Wisdom Mountain* (*Tibetan Meditation Music*)	5:16
Track 9:	Universal Love* (*Universal Love*)	6:44

*Original album

Running time 50 minutes / ℗ & © 2010 Nawang Khechog
All Rights Reserved. No part of this download may be used or reproduced in any manner without written permission from the artist. Visit www.nawangkhechog.com.

 souNDs TruE Music courtesy of Sounds True, Inc.
413 S. Arthur Ave., Louisville, CO 80027
www.soundstrue.com